The navigator of a vessel at Dead Reckoning position 58°10′W takes a sight of the sun's lower limb. The time of the sight is August 1973, 8d 14h 27m 05s GMT. The measured altitude is 57°11′. The index error is 05′ off the arc, and the height of eye is 10 feet.

1973 Aug 8d 14h 27m 05s

Sun	*hs*	57°11′LL
	IC	+05′
	Dip	−03′
	App. Alt.	57°13′
	R-SD	+15′
	Ho	57°28′

1973 Aug	*GHA*	*Dec*
8d – 14h	28°36′	16°05′N
27m– 05s	6°46′	
	35°22′	16°05′N

a λ   58°22′W   *Tab Dec*   16° *Same*

MA   23°E   *Tab Hc*   57°21′   *d* + 51′   *Z N136°E*

aL   42°N   *cor'n*   +04′

                Hc   57°25′   *a = 3T*

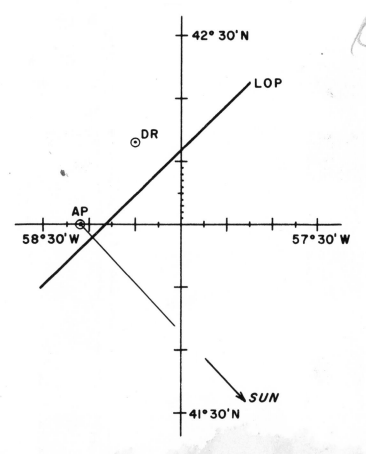

SKY AND SEXTANT
PRACTICAL CELESTIAL NAVIGATION

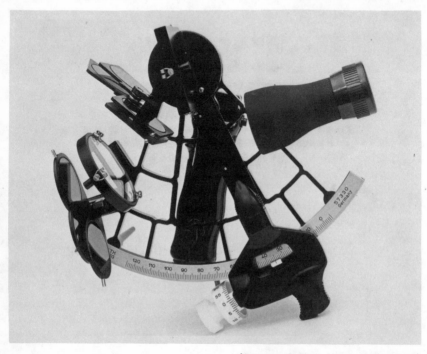

(Courtesy C. Plath, Hamburg, Germany)

SKY AND SEXTANT
PRACTICAL CELESTIAL NAVIGATION

JOHN P. BUDLONG

Musquodoboit Harbour, Nova Scotia

VNR **VAN NOSTRAND REINHOLD COMPANY**
NEW YORK   CINCINNATI   TORONTO   LONDON   MELBOURNE

Van Nostrand Reinhold Company Regional Offices:
New York   Cincinnati   Chicago   Millbrae   Dallas

Van Nostrand Reinhold Company International Offices:
London   Toronto   Melbourne

Library of Congress Catalog Number: 75-12538
ISBN: 0-442-21140-6

Manufactured in the United States of America

Published by Van Nostrand Reinhold Company
450 West 33rd Street, New York, N.Y.   10001

Published simultaneously in Canada by Van Nostrand Reinhold Ltd.

15 14 13 12 11 10 9 8 7 6 5 4 3 2 1

Library of Congress Cataloging in Publication Data
Budlong, John P.   1942-
   Sky and sextant.

   Includes index.
   1. Navigation.   2. Nautical astronomy.   3. Sextant.   I. Title.
VK555.B83   623.89   75-12538
ISBN 0-442-21140-6

Contents

Introduction

Before I bought <u>Pagan</u> I used to think one had to know differential calculus to navigate a peanut across a dishpan. Too, I had looked at Bowditch, Dutton, and Cugle's and walked away blubbering to myself in a navigational fog.

John Caldwell, *Desperate Voyage*

In every ocean port and harbor where there are boats, there are also sailors who would like to venture out of sight of land. They may have been on the water for years, starting with rowboats as kids and gradually working up to bigger craft. They may have bought a boat only recently. In either case, they have done enough sailing and cruising to get to know their boat, and learn basic seamanship, chart reading, and coastwise piloting. In sight of land they are able and confident, and they would cruise offshore but for one factor. Navigation. In particular, celestial navigation. As some people know, "celestial" involves measuring the angle of the sun above the horizon. As many people know, this is done with a mysterious-looking sextant. And as nearly everybody knows, the whole business is complicated, highly mathematical, and very difficult. Even a glance at some of the textbooks available on the subject is enough to confirm their worst fears. True?

Not true. The methods of celestial navigation used today are simple enough to be learned by anyone with enough common sense to sail a boat and read a chart. The mystique of navigation as a complicated black art may have a few roots in the procedures used a good many years ago. Such procedures were longer and more tedious, though not really more difficult. Primarily, though, the idea of difficulty continues to flourish today because the majority of books on the subject *look* complicated. They contain a wealth of detail that is interesting to the practiced navigator, but tremendously confusing to the beginner.

The purpose of this book is to explain the methods of celestial navigation in the clearest and simplest terms. No complicated equations or formulas will be used; math books have more than enough of these. Only addition and subtraction will be required. No advanced or specialized methods will be dealt with; many books of this nature are available to the unusually curious person. Elaborate three-dimensional drawings will not be used, since they are not used in day-to-day navigation. Rules will not be set forth to be learned by rote; the workings of the process will be explained so that you will know what you are doing, and know that you know. Of this is confidence born.

Some people may ask whether, in this day of electronic marvels, celestial navigation really has advantages for the sailor. Yes, there are many advantages. Electronic equipment is expensive. Even a moderately accurate direction-finding receiver, for example, will cost many hundreds of dollars. Its installation will cost something more, and maintenance is yet another expense. The operating power required will have ramifications and complications. Anyone who has spent a perfect sailing day working head-down in the bilges, trying to wrestle loose the corroded connections of a dead battery, in order to replace the battery so that the engine will start, whereby the new battery will stay charged and run the radio, only to discover that the generator brushes are worn out and no spares are on board, will know what I mean. Damp salt air is extremely hostile to many of the components, leading to breakdowns at the most untimely moments. Most electronic aids to navigation depend on transmitters or beacons. Since these are subject to change, it's necessary to keep current on "Notices to Mariners," which list the changes, and this can become a time-consuming chore. Finally, most of the electronic aids have short range. The man who cruises far offshore may soon find that he has no aids at all.

The simplicity of celestial navigation is in sharp contrast. An adequate sextant can be bought new for $12. This, combined with a good timepiece and a set of tables worth $6, will locate your position anywhere on the face of the earth. No power is required. You can navigate in a dinghy as well as in the largest vessel. Along with these practical advantages comes a deep and fundamental satisfaction. You are making your peace with the sea and sky, free from a clutter of modern gadgetry. With your own knowledge and the eternal sky, you are free to sail where you will.

John P. Budlong
Musquodoboit Harbour, Nova Scotia

1 Fundamental Concepts

> *The old Polynesians were great navigators. They took bearings by the sun by day and the stars by night. Their knowledge of the heavenly bodies was astonishing. They knew that the earth was round, and they had names for such abstruse concepts as the Equator and the northern and southern tropics. ... The Polynesians knew five planets, which they called wandering stars, and distinguished them from the fixed stars, for which they had nearly two hundred names.*
>
> Thor Heyerdahl, *Kon-Tiki*

Our earth is spherical, or very nearly so, and this is a good thing. Were it flat, as early geographers believed, there would be no science of celestial navigation as we know it. Our practice of navigation is entirely based on the fact that the "sky" — the sun, moon, planets, and stars — has a different appearance to observers at different points on the earth's curved surface.

Take a mental step into space for a moment, and visualize our rotating earth with the light from the faraway sun shining on one side. Or, if you like your visualizations in smaller sizes, consider a rotating globe with a flashlight shining on it. In either case, it is easily seen that at some point on the surface, the light is shining straight down. As the earth turns, other points move into this position, but at any instant, some one point has the light shining straight down on it. Looked at from another point of view, a person at this spot on the earth's surface would see the sun directly overhead, and he would cast no shadow. Now, it has long been our habit to consider the earth as stationary, with the sun rotating around it. This concept is equally useful to our purposes. We can still realize that at any moment, some point on earth has the sun directly overhead. We call this point the *geographic position* (GP) of the sun. The GP is obviously moving continuously, and rather rapidly at that. Its movement is constant, however, so astronomers are able to predict far in advance the location of the GP at a particular time. This information is published in the *Nautical Almanac,* as we shall presently see.

Figure 1-1 shows the earth as seen from the North Pole, with the sun's rays shining on it. The rays are drawn parallel, which is valid because the sun is so far away compared with the earth's size. (In fact, the distance to the sun is about 12,000 times the earth's diameter.) We'll consider a particular instant of time when the sun's GP is located at point *A.* As discussed above, a person at *A* would see the sun directly overhead. Naturally, a person at *B* will not see the sun at all; for him the sky is dark. At points *C* and *D,* the sun will be visible, but it won't be overhead. Since a person near the earth's surface can see only a tiny portion of the surface, it appears nearly flat, as represented here by a straight line. Notice that at point *D* the sun's rays are parallel to the horizon. A person at *D,* then, would see the sun just on the horizon. At *C,* the sun would appear to be halfway between the horizon and straight overhead; in other words, at an angle of 45° above the horizon.

Run through this again quickly. At the GP, the sun is overhead, or 90 degrees above the horizon. Some distance away from the GP, the sun is 45 degrees above the horizon. Even farther away from the GP, the sun is 0 degrees above the horizon. In other words, *the farther from the GP a*

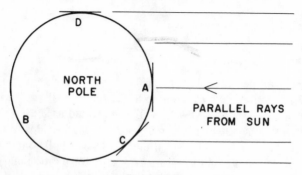

Figure 1-1.

person is, the closer to the horizon he sees the sun. Think about this a bit. It's an important concept. In fact, it's the central concept to all of celestial navigation, and here is the reason. *If you measure the angle of the sun above the horizon, you immediately know how far from the GP you are.* Since we can look up the position of the GP in the Almanac, it's evident that we're well on the way to finding our own position.

Suppose, then, that you measure the angle of the sun above the horizon (the *altitude*), and find it is 54°. It follows that your distance from the GP is 90° – 54°, or 36°. As we will presently see, one degree equals 60 nautical miles, so your distance from the GP must be 36 x 60, or 2160 nautical miles. You look in the Almanac to find the position of the GP at the time you observed the sun. Plot this position on a chart, and draw a circle with a radius of 2160 nautical miles around it. This is your *circle of position;* you are located somewhere on it, though you don't yet know just where on it. The situation is shown in Figure 1-2.

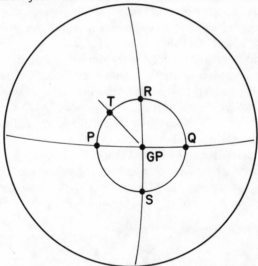

Figure 1-2. The circle of position (P-Q-R-S).

Just where on that circle are you? Suppose for a moment you are at position *P.* You would see the sun to the east of you. If you were at *Q,* the sun would be west. At *R* or *S,* the sun would be south or north, respectively. Now, if the sun is southeast of you, the GP is also southeast of you, so you are northwest of the GP. Draw a line from the GP in a northwest direction until it crosses the circle of position at *T.* This intersection is your position. Not so hard, is it?

This method is useful as an illustration of the basic procedure in finding your position, but it is seldom used in practice. You will probably never use it. The reasons are purely practical. First of all, there is no good way of measuring the direction of the sun with the accuracy needed. Second, while it's fine to talk about a circle with a 2160-mile radius, drawing the circle is something else again. Even if you had a chart covering a big enough area, the circle wouldn't be round, due to the distortions necessary in showing a spherical earth on a flat chart. What you can do, though, is *draw a small part* of the circle of position. Suppose in this case you draw a section of the circle 30 miles long. This 30-mile arc, with a radius of 2160 miles, will have a curvature of less than one degree from one end to the other. A curvature this small can be represented by a straight line without introducing an error large enough to bother with. Now we have the basic method of celestial navigation. We measure the altitude of the sun above the horizon. From the altitude of the sun and the known position of the GP, we calculate the circle of position, and plot a small part of it. This small part is called the *line of position* (LOP).

Chapters 2, 3, 5, 6, 7, and 8 cover the details of these steps, enabling you to take a sextant sight, and work out and plot the line of position. Chapters 9 and 10 deal with refinements of the basic technique. These are not essential, but are often very useful. Chapter 4 explains the arrangement and use of an artificial horizon. This is an important device, enabling you to measure the true altitude of any object, independent of the ocean or horizon. You can thus learn new techniques or practice known ones, even if you live far from the sea.

2 The Line of Position

No aspect of the sailor's world is more mysterious to the landsman than the practice of navigation. To find a precise point in the trackless waste seems neither art nor science, but magic.

Carleton Mitchell, *Passage East*

You'll remember from Chapter 1 that the basic process of celestial navigation is to observe the sun, and from this information obtain a line of position. Now we'll look at the system for describing the position of a point on the earth's surface, and discuss the basic steps of plotting a line of position (LOP).

Distances north or south are measured from the equator, which runs horizontally around the center of the earth. The figures are not expressed in miles, but in *degrees of latitude*. The angle represented can be easily visualized if you imagine the earth to be hollow, with a string stretched from the center to the point in question, and another string stretched to the equator directly under the point. The angle between the strings equals the latitude of the point. If you drew lines around the earth at every 15 degrees of latitude, you would have parallel bands equally spaced from the equator to the poles, as shown in Figure 2-1. The equal spacing is an important concept, because it means that every degree of latitude represents the same distance. The earth has a circumference of 21,600 nautical miles, and since a whole circle contains

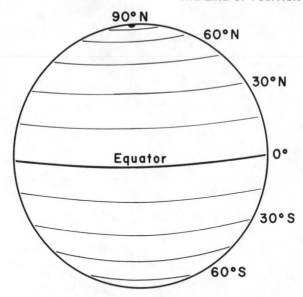

Figure 2-1. Parallels of latitude.

360 degrees, one degree of latitude equals 60 nautical miles. This fact is most useful to navigators; you will be meeting it again. One very handy feature is that you don't need a scale of miles to measure distance on a chart. Every chart has a latitude scale up both sides. To measure any distance, simply refer to this scale. Degrees of latitude are divided for convenience into 60 equal parts, called minutes of latitude. These are represented on the latitude scale by alternate black and white bands. Since there are 60 minutes per degree, it is readily seen that one minute of latitude (one black band or one white band) equals one nautical mile.

Note here that a nautical mile is a bit longer than a statute (land) mile. It equals 6076 feet, compared with the familiar 5280 feet of a statute mile. Whenever a mile is referred to, in this book or in any navigational situation, it is always understood to be a nautical mile. Related to this is the *knot,* a measure of speed. One knot equals one nautical mile per hour. The knot isn't a distance unit, and the sometimes-heard term knots per hour is a misnomer. Distances east and west are expressed in *degrees of longitude.* Lines of longitude run from the north pole to the south, crossing the equator at right angles. If you drew lines at every 15 degrees of longitude, they would cross the equator at equal distances, and meet at the poles. There's a strong resemblence to the segments of a peeled orange, as shown in Figure 2-2.

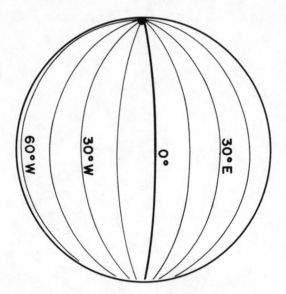

Figure 2-2. Lines of longitude.

Since the lines of longitude converge at the poles, their spacing depends on the distance from the equator, and we cannot say that a degree of longitude equals any particular distance. As a result, the longitude scales across the top and bottom of a chart must not be used to measure distance.

Just as we use the equator for measuring latitude, we must have a starting point for measuring longitude. By international agreement, this is the line of longitude which runs through the original site of the observatory at Greenwich, England. As lines of longitude are also called *meridians,* this one is often called the prime meridian. Longitude is measured east or west from the prime meridian to a maximum of 180 degrees.

Now that we've got some basic terms under our belts, what about that line of position? If the sun happens (either through chance or through planning) to be due east or west of us, or due north or south, plotting the LOP is dead simple. For example, let's say that about noon you observe the sun, which is due south. It's altitude is 55°. From your almanac you find that the sun's *declination* (latitude of the GP) at this time is 17°N. Your latitude, then, is figured simply as $(90^\circ - 55^\circ) + 17^\circ = 52^\circ$N. Draw a horizontal line on your chart at latitude 52°N, and this is your LOP. Done. I think you'll agree that this is a simple procedure.

It's so simple, in fact, that taking a noon sight for latitude is a time-honored tradition even to this day. We'll cover this type of LOP in a later chapter which will explain, among other things, why we subtracted 55° from 90°, and why we added 17°.

Simple and useful as it may be, this method alone is not enough to navigate by, for the obvious reason that the sun is not usually so co-operative as to be due east, west, north, or south. We need another system, which can reckon with the sun's being in any direction and at any altitude. Let's assume that a vessel, not our own, is at position A in Figure 2-3, off Cape Sable, Nova Scotia. The latitude is 43°N, and the longitude is 65°W.

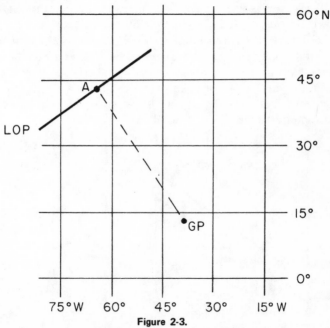

Figure 2-3.

The existence of this other vessel is a temporary assumption only, as will presently be seen. Let's also assume that the sun's GP at this time is 13°N, 39°W. From these four figures, it is possible to calculate the sun's altitude, as it would be observed from the vessel at A. This calculation used to be a lengthy and tedious job, involving such frightening-sounding terms as log haversine, natural cosine, and so forth. These days, however, mathematicians have done all the calculations for us, and we simply look up the answer in a table. (This is covered in detail in

Chapter 7.) In this case we look in the table and find that the navigator at A would observe the sun at an altitude of 52°33′. We also find that the sun's direction would be southeast, which certainly seems reasonable when you look at the plot. (Note: All directions and bearings relating to celestial navigation are "true," measured from geographic north as shown on the chart. This will differ from magnetic north by the amount of variation that exists at the location.) Now draw a line through A, running perpendicular to the sun's direction. This is A's LOP. It is a small part of the circle of position centered at the sun's GP.

Now we come sailing along in the same vicinity as A, perhaps 10 miles away. This is so close to A, compared with the distance to the GP (2247 miles in this case, but not something we normally work out) that we will also see the sun in a southeast direction. Suppose it happens that we observe the sun's altitude to be 52°33′, the same altitude that the navigator at A observed. This can only mean that we are on the same LOP as the vessel at A. We might be located at position B, or at C, as shown in Figure 2-4. At the moment we don't know which. But we *do* know that we are on A's LOP, and so we have found our *own* LOP. Please note that these plots are not drawn to scale.

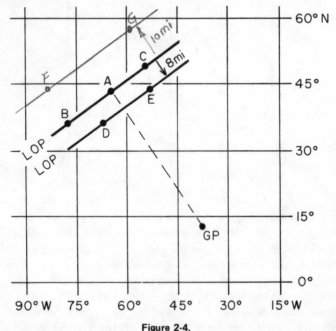

Figure 2-4.

Suppose it happens that we do *not* observe the sun's altitude to be 52°33', as *A* did. (In actual practice we generally don't, in fact.) We then realize that we are not located on *A*'s LOP, since a navigator at any point on that LOP would observe the same altitude as *A*. Suppose we observe the altitude as 52°41'. You'll recall from Chapter 1 that the closer we are to the sun's GP, the greater the observed altitude. You'll also recall that one minute of arc equals one mile. Since we observed the sun's altitude to be 8 minutes of arc greater than *A*'s navigator, we must be located 8 miles closer to the sun's GP. We can still say, though, that we are very close to *A* compared with our distance from the sun's GP. Therefore we will observe the sun in the same direction as *A*. We can then plot our LOP by measuring 8 miles from *A* toward the GP, marking the point, and drawing a perpendicular through the point. We are located somewhere on this LOP, perhaps at *D*, perhaps at *E*, but not, except by coincidence, at the intersection of the LOP with the line from *A* to the GP.

Suppose that *A* and the sun are still in the same position as before, and we are somewhere in the vicinity of *A*, but we observe the sun's altitude to be 52°23'. We know that the farther we move from the GP the lower will be the observed altitude. Since we observe the sun at a lower altitude than *A*, we must be farther away. Since the altitude is 10 minutes of arc less, the distance from *A* must be 10 miles. We then measure 10 miles from *A* away from the GP, and draw our LOP as a perpendicular, as shown in Figure 2-5.

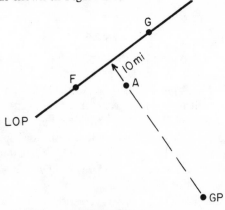

Figure 2-5.

We are located on this LOP, perhaps at *F* or *G*. Notice that in this plot *A*'s position is drawn, but not its LOP. This is the usual practice, since it makes a simpler plot. One less line means one less possible error.

For another example, consider a vessel at position A in Figure 2-6, off the coast of Queen Charlotte Island, British Columbia. The latitude is 52°N. The longitude is 137°W. The GP of the sun at this time is 19°N, 166°W, somewhat west of Honolulu. From the tables we find that the observed altitude at A will be 49°58', and the bearing from A will be southwest. From our own vessel, some distance from A, we observe the sun's altitude to be 50°18'. Since the sun's altitude is 20 minutes of arc greater at our position than at A's position, we know that we are 20 miles closer to the GP. To plot our LOP, then, we measure 20 miles from A toward the GP (southwest) and draw the perpendicular. This is our LOP.

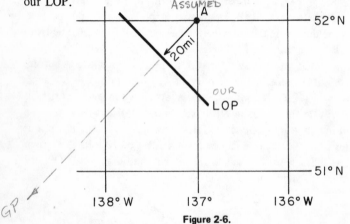

Figure 2-6.

This example is typical. We have plotted A's position, the direction toward the GP, and our own LOP. This is the usual practice in plotting LOP's. We have not plotted A's LOP, or the actual position of the GP. The reason for omitting A's LOP, as before, is simplicity in the plot. The reason for not plotting the sun's actual GP is a practical one. If we used a chart of such small scale that both British Columbia and Honolulu were shown, it would be impossible to plot accurately the relatively tiny 14 miles involved in our LOP. Also, an LOP drawn on such a chart would not lend itself to accurate use.

Consider for a moment the vessel at position A. We have <u>assumed</u> that a vessel is there, and accordingly looked up in tables the altitude at which the sun would be observed there. The vessel, though, has been just a <u>useful fiction</u>. It really needn't be there, and in fact really isn't there.

The only vessel in the neighborhood is our own. We simply assume the position of A in order to find the sun's calculated altitude and bearing there, which we compare with our own observed altitude and thus plot our own LOP. The position of the imaginary vessel A is called an assumed position (AP). We *could* locate the AP any place within 20 or 30 miles of our own position, but in practice there are certain guidelines for choosing the AP.

These examples have illustrated the basic method of finding our LOP. The steps in the process are:

1. Measure the observed altitude of the sun and note the time.

2. Using the Almanac, find the GP of the sun at the time of our observation.

3. Choose an AP, and use tables to find the calculated altitude of the sun at the AP.

4. Compare the observed altitude with the calculated altitude, and plot the LOP.

The method, I hope you'll agree, is simple. Each of the steps above is explained in detail in the following chapters.

3 The Sextant

Cadet von Zartowsky took odds and ends and made a sextant that afterward took us fifty nautical miles off our course, pretty fair, considering the circumstances.

Lowell Thomas, *Count Luckner, The Sea Devil*

The first job in finding your LOP is to measure the angle, or altitude, of the sun above the horizon. Over the years, a number of interesting devices have been used for this measurement. Possibly one of the earliest seagoing versions was a cuplike affair which was used in the Pacific islands. The cup had holes spaced around the side. It was filled with water up to the holes, and the navigator made his measurement by sighting over the rim. Later developments included the *cross-staff*, a sticklike device, and the more compact *astrolabe*, which has recently seen use on the Nina II expedition. The instrument in common use today, of course, is the sextant. The name is derived from the Latin *sextans*, or sixth part of a circle. Due to the arrangement of the optics, the sextant will actually measure angles up to one third of a circle, or 120 degrees. You may also still encounter the sextant's earlier cousins, the quadrant and the octant.

Although a sextant looks pretty complicated at first glance, it really has just three basic parts. A telescope or sighting device for looking at the horizon. An adjustable mirror, enabling one to see the sun as well as the horizon. A scale graduated in degrees and minutes, from which one reads the sun's altitude. You very possibly already own a sextant, and are reading this book for some pointers in using it. For the benefit of those who are about to buy one, though, I offer the following comments.

Sextants can be bought in a wide variety of models. The cheapest costs about 15 dollars and gives quite satisfactory results. At the other end of the range, it's no trick to pay hundreds of dollars for a truly precision instrument. They all work on the same principle and are used in about the same way. The main differences are in accuracy, which is really not a great concern, and the ease of use, which is. Let me explain this apparently contradictory statement. When taking sights at sea, a variety of possible errors may creep into the process, quite apart from sextant accuracy. In the final result, an uncertainty of two miles in the LOP is considered quite acceptable, and an uncertainty of 10 miles may be expected in some circumstances. In this context, a sextant error of a mile or so is hardly worth worrying about. On the other hand, it proves only too easy to make a good old-fashioned mistake, and if the sextant is awkward to use or to read, so much the more likely. Reading the angle as $37°28'$, for example, when the actual angle is $38°28'$, will put your LOP off by 60 miles. This is definitely something to avoid!

Your choice may be dictated largely by your finances. Even if price isn't important, though, I'd suggest that you consider the advantages of the inexpensive plastic sextants. Along with low price, they have the distinct advantage of being lightweight. You'll really appreciate this feature if you spend half an hour or so taking practice sights; a traditional brass sextant will have your arm aching and shaking, but the burden of a plastic one will hardly be noticed. On the average, the plastic models come in smaller carrying cases, which really helps the stowage problem on a small boat. The parts are also corrosion-resistant, although salt water on the mirrors should be rinsed off, as with any sextant.

Plastic sextants are made by Davis, in California, and by Ebbco, in England. Both are distributed through dealers in nautical instruments. Davis makes an economy model for $13. Both companies make models in the $50 range. The latter have some extra features and better accuracy, making them a good choice in many cases.

Avoid the most expensive instruments, even if your finances are unlimited. The superb accuracy of these is quite unnecessary with a small boat, and they are works of such beauty and precision that you'd hesitate to even take one near salt water or dirt or where it might get bumped. This takes half the fun out of a fascinating art.

You should fit your sextant with a lanyard of strong nylon cord, and keep this around your neck whenever using the sextant. This will prevent a catastrophe should you lose your grip; a sextant dropped on deck is a sextant ruined, and a sextant dropped overboard floats very poorly indeed!

Try out the instrument before buying. It should have a comfortable heft. Adjust it through its whole range, to see if the mechanism works smoothly and easily. Check that both mirrors have adjusting screws. Look (not through a glass door or window) at some distant horizontal line: a tanker's waterline, a rooftop, power lines, or whatever. This object should appear in the sextant split into two segments, which move relative to each other. See Figure 3-1(a) and 3-1(b). Adjust the image to appear as one unbroken line, as in Figure 3-1(c), and then read the angle. The reading should be zero or near to it, preferably within 10 or 15 minutes. Don't worry if you find a small error; you can either live with it, or adjust it later.

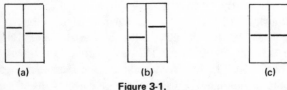

| (a) | (b) | (c) |

Figure 3-1.

A word of caution here about bubble sextants. You may find one of these on the surplus market. They are intended for use on aircraft, using a small bubble instead of the visible horizon. On board a boat the bubble will dance about, making readings impossible.

MEASURING THE SUN'S ALTITUDE

What we want to do, of course, is measure the angle between the horizon and the sun's center. Since it isn't feasible to locate the exact center, we measure instead to the lower edge, and add a correction later. If you can take your sextant to a beach where the horizon beneath the sun is visible, that is fine. Otherwise, though, the rooftop across the street will make a good makeshift horizon. First put the darkest shade in place between the index and horizon mirrors, to protect your eye against a direct look at the sun. Set the index arm to zero. Now look through the telescope at the horizon, in the direction of the sun. Swing the index arm slowly away from you toward middle readings on the scale, and presently the sun will come into view in the telescope, moving down as you swing the index arm out. Keep adjusting until the bottom edge (the *lower limb*) of the sun appears to just touch the horizon. This is called *bringing down* the sun. Now you have to check that you're using the part of the horizon directly under the sun. To do this, imagine an axis through the telescope. Slowly swing the sextant back and forth around this axis, and the sun will appear to swing from side to side in a gentle arc (see Figure 3-2).

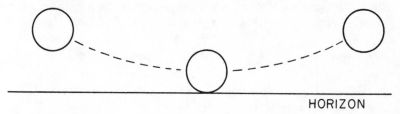

HORIZON

Figure 3-2.

When the sun is at the lowest part of the arc, you are aimed at the right spot on the horizon, and can make the final adjustment. At sea, the sun's glare on the water often helps show the right spot. Reading the angle on the sextant's scale now gives the altitude of the sun's lower limb above the horizon. Practice this several times until it becomes quite natural and easy. In the process, you'll notice that successive readings will change, increasing if the sun is in the east (rising), or decreasing if the sun is in the west (setting).

READING THE SCALE

The main scale on your sextant, the arc, is graduated to read degrees directly. All types of marine sextants have nearly identical arcs, with every degree marked and every tenth degree numbered. To read minutes of angle, two types of device are in use. The more common today is the micrometer drum, which is graduated to read directly in minutes. A reading of this type is so simple as to need no explanation, other than the remark that you first read the number of whole degrees on the main arc, using the smaller figure to the right of the index mark, and then add the number of minutes as read from the drum. If your sextant comes equipped with a drum vernier, a small scale (usually five divisions) next to the drum for reading fractions of a minute, ignore it. Simply read the drum to the nearest minute.

Many older sextants, and the cheaper models being made today, come equipped with a tangent vernier. This simple device is located beside the main arc scale, and allows readings to a minute of arc (two minutes on some models) without resorting to the delicate and expensive worm gear of the micrometer drum. The vernier scale has a number of uniformly spaced marks. The right-hand of these, marked 0, is the index mark, used to read degrees on the main scale. Having read the degrees on the main scale, look along the vernier scale to find a mark which is exactly opposite a mark on the main scale. The minute value of this mark on the vernier scale is added to the number of degrees on the main scale to give the angle. Figure 3-3 illustrates a reading of 15°24′.

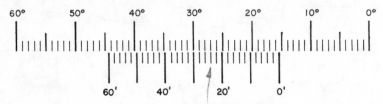

Figure 3-3.   A reading of 15°24′.

CORRECTIONS TO THE READING

The angle read from the sextant is written down with the label *hs,* for height-sextant. We noted above that we must add a correction to give the true angle of the sun's center. There are also a couple of other small corrections to be applied. The result of the corrections is the true altitude of the center of the sun, and is written with the label *Ho,* for height-observed. The first correction to be applied is the index correction (IC) and is simply the reverse of the index error discussed earlier. After taking your sun sight and writing down the angle, set the sextant back to zero. Swing back the sunshade and look at the horizon. Adjust the index arm until the horizon appears as an unbroken line. Read the angle. If it is 0, you have no index error and no IC to apply. (Note: Using a nearby object will introduce an apparent index error where there may actually be none. Use an object at least half a mile away.) If the angle is slightly more than zero, you have an index error *on the arc,* and the IC must be taken *off* the reading of hs. If the angle is slightly less than zero, you have an index error *off the arc,* and the IC must be added *on* the reading of hs. When reading an angle off the arc, the vernier figures must be read in the reverse direction. This is easy with a drum vernier, but wants watching with a tangent vernier. Figure 3-4 shows an index error of 14′ off the arc. To keep the corrections straight, just remember the old seagoing saw: If you're on, you're off; but if you're off, you're on.

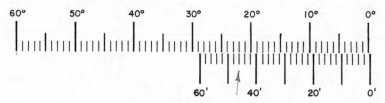

Figure 3-4. Index error 14′ off the arc.

The second correction to be applied is dip, usually abbreviated D. When you take a sight using the sea horizon, your eye is at least a few feet above the surface. Since the earth is curved, this means that you are actually looking *down* at the visible horizon, rather than straight out in a truly horizontal direction. As a result, your reading of hs is too large, and the dip correction must always be subtracted. Figure 3-5 shows the situation.

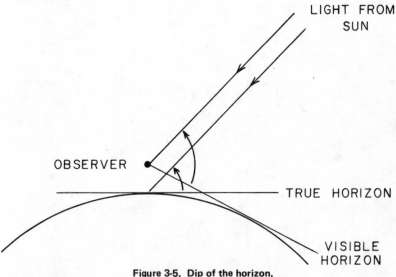

Figure 3-5. Dip of the horizon.

A table of dip corrections, accurate to the nearest tenth of a minute, is given on the inside front cover of the almanac, and reproduced here as Table 1. The height of eye is given in both meters and feet. The correction should be rounded off to the nearest minute. For example, if your height of eye is 6 feet, the dip correction is -2′. If your height of eye is 10 feet, the dip correction is -3′. A handy rule of thumb is that the square root of the height of eye, in feet, gives the dip correction, in minutes. Thus, a height of eye of 25 feet requires a correction of -5′.

Table 1.

A2 ALTITUDE CORRECTION TABLES 10°–90°—SUN, STARS, PLANETS

SUN OCT.–MAR. / SUN APR.–SEPT.

App. Alt.	Lower Limb	Upper Limb	App. Alt.	Lower Limb	Upper Limb
9 34	+10.8	−21.5	9 39	+10.6	−21.2
9 45	+10.9	−21.4	9 51	+10.7	−21.1
9 56	+11.0	−21.3	10 03	+10.8	−21.0
10 08	+11.1	−21.2	10 15	+10.9	−20.9
10 21	+11.2	−21.1	10 27	+11.0	−20.8
10 34	+11.3	−21.0	10 40	+11.1	−20.7
10 47	+11.4	−20.9	10 54	+11.2	−20.6
11 01	+11.5	−20.8	11 08	+11.3	−20.5
11 15	+11.6	−20.7	11 23	+11.4	−20.4
11 30	+11.7	−20.6	11 38	+11.5	−20.3
11 46	+11.8	−20.5	11 54	+11.6	−20.2
12 02	+11.9	−20.4	12 10	+11.7	−20.1
12 19	+12.0	−20.3	12 28	+11.8	−20.0
12 37	+12.1	−20.2	12 46	+11.9	−19.9
12 55	+12.2	−20.1	13 05	+12.0	−19.8
13 14	+12.3	−20.0	13 24	+12.1	−19.7
13 35	+12.4	−19.9	13 45	+12.2	−19.6
13 56	+12.5	−19.8	14 07	+12.3	−19.5
14 18	+12.6	−19.7	14 30	+12.4	−19.4
14 42	+12.7	−19.6	14 54	+12.5	−19.3
15 06	+12.8	−19.5	15 19	+12.6	−19.2
15 32	+12.9	−19.4	15 46	+12.7	−19.1
15 59	+13.0	−19.3	16 14	+12.8	−19.0
16 28	+13.1	−19.2	16 44	+12.9	−18.9
16 59	+13.2	−19.1	17 15	+13.0	−18.8
17 32	+13.3	−19.0	17 48	+13.1	−18.7
18 06	+13.4	−18.9	18 24	+13.2	−18.6
18 42	+13.5	−18.8	19 01	+13.3	−18.5
19 21	+13.6	−18.7	19 42	+13.4	−18.4
20 03	+13.7	−18.6	20 25	+13.5	−18.3
20 48	+13.8	−18.5	21 11	+13.6	−18.2
21 35	+13.9	−18.4	22 00	+13.7	−18.1
22 26	+14.0	−18.3	22 54	+13.8	−18.0
23 22	+14.1	−18.2	23 51	+13.9	−17.9
24 21	+14.2	−18.1	24 53	+14.0	−17.8
25 26	+14.3	−18.0	26 00	+14.1	−17.7
26 36	+14.4	−17.9	27 13	+14.2	−17.6
27 52	+14.5	−17.8	28 33	+14.3	−17.5
29 15	+14.6	−17.7	30 00	+14.4	−17.4
30 46	+14.7	−17.6	31 35	+14.5	−17.3
32 26	+14.8	−17.5	33 20	+14.6	−17.2
34 17	+14.9	−17.4	35 17	+14.7	−17.1
36 20	+15.0	−17.3	37 26	+14.8	−17.0
38 36	+15.1	−17.2	39 50	+14.9	−16.9
41 08	+15.2	−17.1	42 31	+15.0	−16.8
43 59	+15.3	−17.0	45 31	+15.1	−16.7
47 10	+15.4	−16.9	48 55	+15.2	−16.6
50 46	+15.5	−16.8	52 44	+15.3	−16.5
54 49	+15.6	−16.7	57 02	+15.4	−16.4
59 23	+15.7	−16.6	61 51	+15.5	−16.3
64 30	+15.8	−16.5	67 17	+15.6	−16.2
70 12	+15.9	−16.4	73 16	+15.7	−16.1
76 26	+16.0	−16.3	79 43	+15.8	−16.0
83 05	+16.1	−16.2	86 32	+15.9	−15.9
90 00			90 00		

STARS AND PLANETS

App. Alt.	Corrn
9 56	−5.3
10 08	−5.2
10 20	−5.1
10 33	−5.0
10 46	−4.9
11 00	−4.8
11 14	−4.7
11 29	−4.6
11 45	−4.5
12 01	−4.4
12 18	−4.3
12 35	−4.2
12 54	−4.1
13 13	−4.0
13 33	−3.9
13 54	−3.8
14 16	−3.7
14 40	−3.6
15 04	−3.5
15 30	−3.4
15 57	−3.3
16 26	−3.2
16 56	−3.1
17 28	−3.0
18 02	−2.9
18 38	−2.8
19 17	−2.7
19 58	−2.6
20 42	−2.5
21 28	−2.4
22 19	−2.3
23 13	−2.2
24 11	−2.1
25 14	−2.0
26 22	−1.9
27 36	−1.8
28 56	−1.7
30 24	−1.6
32 00	−1.5
33 45	−1.4
35 40	−1.3
37 48	−1.2
40 08	−1.1
42 44	−1.0
45 36	−0.9
48 47	−0.8
52 18	−0.7
56 11	−0.6
60 28	−0.5
65 08	−0.4
70 11	−0.3
75 34	−0.2
81 13	−0.1
87 03	0.0
90 00	

Additional Corrn — 1973

App. Alt.	Corrn
VENUS	
Jan. 1 – Sept. 30	
0° 42	+0.1
Oct. 1 – Nov. 15	
0° 47	+0.2
Nov. 16 – Dec. 12	
0° 46	+0.3
Dec. 13 – Dec. 28	
0° 11	+0.4
41	+0.5
Dec. 29 – Dec. 31	
0° 6	+0.5
20	+0.6
31	+0.7
MARS	
Jan. 1 – June 14	
0° 60	+0.1
June 15 – Aug. 26	
0° 41	+0.2
75	+0.1
Aug. 27 – Nov. 28	
0° 34	+0.3
60	+0.2
80	+0.1
Nov. 29 – Dec. 31	
0° 41	+0.2
75	+0.1

DIP

Ht. of Eye (m)	Corrn	Ht. of Eye (ft)	Corrn	Ht. of Eye (m)	Corrn
2.4	−2.8	8.0		1.0	−1.8
2.6	−2.9	8.6		1.5	−2.2
2.8	−3.0	9.2		2.0	−2.5
3.0	−3.1	9.8		2.5	−2.8
3.2	−3.2	10.5		3.0	−3.0
3.4	−3.3	11.2		See table ←	
3.6	−3.4	11.9		m	
3.8	−3.5	12.6		20	−7.9
4.0	−3.6	13.3		22	−8.3
4.3	−3.7	14.1		24	−8.6
4.5	−3.8	14.9		26	−9.0
4.7	−3.9	15.7		28	−9.3
5.0	−4.0	16.5			
5.2	−4.1	17.4		30	−9.6
5.5	−4.2	18.3		32	−10.0
5.8	−4.3	19.1		34	−10.3
6.1	−4.4	20.1		36	−10.6
6.3	−4.5	21.0		38	−10.8
6.6	−4.6	22.0			
6.9	−4.7	22.9		40	−11.1
7.2	−4.8	23.9		42	−11.4
7.5	−4.9	24.9		44	−11.7
7.9	−5.0	26.0		46	−11.9
8.2	−5.1	27.1		48	−12.2
8.5	−5.2	28.1		ft.	
8.8	−5.3	29.2		2	−1.4
9.2	−5.4	30.4		4	−1.9
9.5	−5.5	31.5		6	−2.4
9.9	−5.6	32.7		8	−2.7
10.3	−5.7	33.9		10	−3.1
10.6	−5.8	35.1		See table ←	
11.0	−5.9	36.3		ft.	
11.4	−6.0	37.6		70	−8.1
11.8	−6.1	38.9		75	−8.4
12.2	−6.2	40.1		80	−8.7
12.6	−6.3	41.5		85	−8.9
13.0	−6.4	42.8		90	−9.2
13.4	−6.5	44.2		95	−9.5
13.8	−6.6	45.5			
14.2	−6.7	46.9		100	−9.7
14.7	−6.8	48.4		105	−9.9
15.1	−6.9	49.8		110	−10.2
15.5	−7.0	51.3		115	−10.4
16.0	−7.1	52.8		120	−10.6
16.5	−7.2	54.3		125	−10.8
16.9	−7.3	55.8			
17.4	−7.4	57.4		130	−11.1
17.9	−7.5	58.9		135	−11.3
18.4	−7.6	60.5		140	−11.5
18.8	−7.7	62.1		145	−11.7
19.3	−7.8	63.8		150	−11.9
19.8	−7.9	65.4		155	−12.1
20.4	−8.0	67.1			
20.9	−8.1	68.8			
21.4		70.5			

App. Alt. = Apparent altitude = Sextant altitude corrected for index error and dip.

At sea, if you can pick a standard place in the boat to take your sights, the dip correction will always be the same. It is even possible to deliberately set the index error to take care of dip, though this is not recommended since the index error may change.

The two remaining corrections to a sun sight are generally combined in a single table. These are refraction and semidiameter. Since we'll meet the Refraction correction again when discussing planet and star sights, I'll explain the two separately and then show how the combined table is used.

Refraction means the bending of light rays as they pass through the earth's atmosphere. By referring to Figure 3-6, you will see that the rays are bent down, with the result that the body looks higher than it actually is. Consequently, the refraction correction (R) is always subtracted.

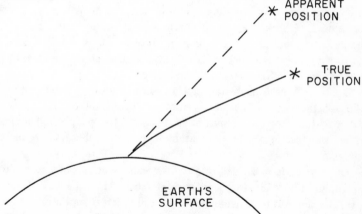

Figure 3-6. The effect of refraction.

If the sun is low in the sky, its rays have a longer, oblique, path through the atmosphere. The bending effect is then more pronounced, and a greater correction must be applied. If the sun is directly overhead, there is no bending of the rays, and the correction is zero. A table of refraction corrections is given on the inside front cover of the Almanac, under the heading "Stars and Planets," incorporated here in Table 1. The table is entered with the apparent altitude (App Alt) of the body (hs corrected for IC and dip), and gives the refraction correction, in minutes and tenths, to be subtracted. Round the correction off to the nearest minute. For example, if the App Alt is 25°30′, the refraction correction is –02′, and the true altitude is 25°28′. Observations with an altitude of less than 10 degrees are generally to be avoided. Occasionally, though, such a sight may be necessary. The refraction correction is then taken from the table on the page facing the inside front cover of the Almanac.

Semidiameter (SD) is the difference in angles measured to the sun's edge and to its center. Since we generally measure the altitude of the lower limb, and the center is obviously higher, we must add the correction. The amount is about 16 minutes of arc.

Suppose, then, we made an observation of the sun's lower limb, and after correcting for IC and dip we had an apparent altitude of 24° 30'. We could subtract the refraction correction of -02', and add the SD correction of +16', for a total correction of +14', giving a true altitude of 24°44'. Since the SD correction doesn't depend on altitude, though, it's easier to combine the two corrections into one. This is the purpose of the table labeled *Sun* on the inside front cover of the Almanac. Refer to Table 1. In this example, if you look in the *Lower Limb* column, the correction corresponding to an App Alt of 24°30' is +13'.9. Rounding to the nearest minute, we have +14', the same as we got by taking the refraction and SD corrections separately.

Occasionally you might take a sight of the sun's upper limb. In this case, take the combined correction from the Upper Limb column. You'll notice that this correction must be subtracted. Most people find adding easier, and that is one of the reasons that lower limb sights are more common.

The *Sun* table is divided into two sections — one from October to March, and the other from April to September. This is because the sun is slightly closer to the earth in winter, which makes it appear bigger and causes a larger SD correction. The difference is just a couple of tenths of a minute, though, so you can forget it and use whichever part of the table you get accustomed to.

These explanations, even though brief, have added up. Lest you get the idea that the correction business is pretty hairy, let's review the steps and see just how simple they are. After taking a lower limb sun sight, you must:

1. Add or subtract the IC, depending on your sextant.

2. Subtract the dip correction.

3. Add the combined Ref-SD correction.

The result is called the observed altitude (Ho). This name, observed altitude, is a bit tricky, since it's *not* the altitude that you actually observe and read from the sextant. It's the altitude that you theoretically would observe if none of the sources of error were present. After applying corrections for these errors, then, we call the result the observed altitude. As a final example, consider a lower limb sun sight, with a sextant reading of 36°10'. The index error is 03' off the arc. The height of eye is 5 feet. The figuring will look like this:

hs	36°10'
IC	+03'
D	–02'
App alt	36°11'
Ref-SD	+15'
Ho	36°26'

And that's that!

Here are some practice problems, all sun sights. The answers are to be found in the Appendix.

1. hs 52°17', lower limb, index error 05' on the arc, height of eye 12 ft

2.   22°57', lower limb,   02' off the arc,   9 ft

3.   72°35', upper limb,   04' on the arc,   10 ft

4.   08°27', lower limb,   11' off the arc,   5 ft

SEXTANT ERRORS AND ADJUSTMENTS

The cheaper models of sextants often need adjusting when first purchased, and any model may require adjustment on occasion, especially if subjected to a lot of vibration. Constant adjustment should be avoided, because it could wear the screw threads. But there's no reason to avoid the job if it needs doing. It's neither difficult nor mysterious. The three most common forms of sextant errors are all adjustable. These are perpendicularity error, side error, and index error. They are adjusted in that order.

Perpendicularity error comes about if the index mirror isn't perpendicular to the plane of the arc. To check this, hold the sextant flat and swing the index arm until you can sight obliquely across the index mirror and see the arc reflected. If the reflection seems to line up with the arc seen directly, no adjustment is needed. If the images are offset, the index mirror must be adjusted (see Figure 3-7). The adjustment is made with the single adjusting screw, on the outside of the mirror bracket. (*Caution:* On some older sextants, each adjusting point has a pair of screws. One must be loosened before the other is tightened.)

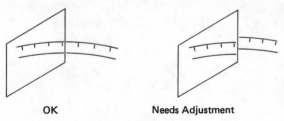

OK   Needs Adjustment

Figure 3-7.

Side error will be present if the horizon glass isn't perpendicular to the plane of the arc. To check this, look at a horizontal line and adjust the index arm to get an unbroken line. Now tip the sextant on an angle. If the line stays unbroken, there is no side error (see Figure 3-8). If adjustment is needed, look on the back of the horizon glass for two screws. The one nearest the frame adjusts the side error.

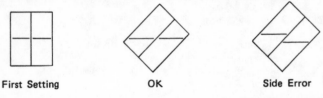

First Setting   OK   Side Error

Figure 3-8.

Another way to detect side error is to look at a star while swinging the index arm past zero. If the two images pass directly over each other, there is no error. If they pass without touching, adjustment is needed (see Figure 3-9).

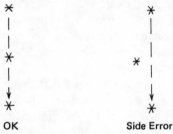

OK   Side Error

Figure 3-9.

The last thing to check is index error. As explained earlier, this simply means that when the images of a faraway object are lined up, the vernier should read zero. (Stated in optical terms, the horizon glass and index mirror must be parallel when the index arm is set to zero.) Pick an object at least half a mile away. This can be a horizontal line, such as a rooftop, if the sextant is held in the normal position. If you turn it on its side, a vertical line like the side of a building can be used. Adjust the vernier carefully for an unbroken line. If the reading is zero, you're all set. If not, the screw on the horizon glass, farthest from the frame, should be adjusted.

4 The Artificial Horizon

At night Teroro . . . would place on the platform near the prow a half coconut, filled with placid sea water, and in it he would catch the reflection of the fixed star, and by keeping this reflection constant in the cup, he maintained his course.

James Michener, *Hawaii*

About now you'll be wanting to try some real sights on the sun. If you live near enough to the sea, and can find a place with a view in a southerly direction, fine. But what if you don't live near the sea, or your only available beach looks toward the north, so that the sun is never over the visible horizon, what then? No panic. You can do all the practice sights you want without leaving your own backyard. These sights can be worked out to give actual LOP's. Comparing these with the actual position of your practice location, as determined from a chart or topographic map, will show whether you're doing things right.

The clue to taking sights when you're not near the sea is a device which I like to call a "$450, parallax-corrected, achromatic, front surface reflecting, self-leveling, dip-corrected, temperature-compensated, portable artificial horizon." This marvelous machine can be used for sights of the sun, moon, planets, or stars. It introduces no errors. (How could it, with a name like that?) Best of all, it won't cost you anything.

Find a container such as a bread pan or soup bowl. Fill it nearly to the top with water, and set it where the sun shines on it. Now move around until you find a place where you can see the reflection of the sun on the surface of the water. (Even the reflection is bright enough to be hard on the eyes; don't look at it long.) Using both sets of shades on your sextant, look through the telescope at the sun's reflected image. This of course will require aiming the sextant downward. Having once found the reflected image in the telescope, move the index arm of the sextant until a second image of the sun comes into view. This image is seen by way of the mirrors on the sextant, so we'll call it the sextant image. You'll find that if you rotate the sextant around that imaginary axis through the telescope, the sextant image will swing from side to side, while the reflected image will remain more or less still. This is the way to tell which is which. You may find it necessary to change the combination of filters so that the two images are about the same intensity. For best results use a dimmer rather than a brighter image. Don't look through the telescope while you're changing filters, lest you catch a glimpse of the sun without any filter.

Once you've got the two images suitably filtered and near each other in the telescope, you're ready for the final adjustment. This requires making the two images just touch each other, lower limb to lower limb. The reflected image is inverted, however, so the lower limb appears uppermost. Figure 4-1 shows how the images will appear in the telescope when correctly adjusted. Again, remember that you can tell which image is which by rocking the sextant.

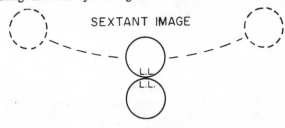

SEXTANT IMAGE

L.L.
L.L.

REFLECTED IMAGE

Figure 4-1.

When you have the final adjustment made, don't forget to note the time, if you're going to use the sight to work out an LOP. The angle on the sextant scales is just twice the angle you would measure with the sea horizon, neglecting corrections for the moment. The basic optical principle involved is that both parts of a reflected light ray make the same angle with the reflecting surface. The situation is shown in Figure 4-2.

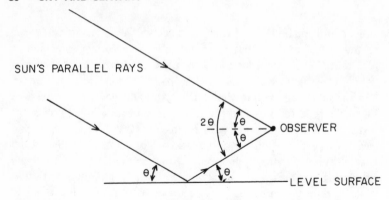

Figure 4-2.

After reading the angle from the scales, determine the index error and apply it to the reading, in just the same fashion as described in Chapter 3. Divide the result by two. This angle is equivalent to a sight with a sea horizon, corrected for index error. Now, a sea-horizon sight would have to be corrected for dip, but an artificial-horizon sight doesn't have to be. The only remaining correction is the refraction-semidiameter value obtained from the "Sun" table. To tie all this together, follow the example below of an artificial horizon sight with an indicated angle of 86°27′ and an index error of 05′ on the arc.

hs	86°27′
IC	−05′
2 App alt	86°22′
App alt	43°11′
Ref-SD	+15′
Ho	43°26′

In the example, the double apparent altitude was an even number of degrees, so the division by two presented no problem. However, if the double apparent altitude is an odd number of degrees, an extra step is needed. I'll illustrate this with the extra step written out; usually you can do it in your head. In this case, the sextant reading is 37°46′, with an index error of 02′ off the arc.

hs	37°46′	
IC	+02′	
2 App alt	37°48′	= 36°108′
App alt		18° 54′
Ref-SD		+13′
Ho		19° 07′

It may strike you as odd that the method of figuring shown here actually involves dividing the IC by two. The reason is that although the measured angle is about twice as large as would be observed with a sea horizon; it's nevertheless just an angle to be measured, and the indicated angle must have the IC applied to give the true angle. Due to the reflection, this is twice the apparent altitude, and so is divided by two.

Using this form of artificial horizon does have one shortcoming. Wind affects it, setting the reflected image to dancing and making the reading difficult or impossible. The problem can usually be avoided by taking sights in the early morning, before the wind gets up. Sometimes evenings are also calm. In case you want to use the artificial horizon when the wind is blowing, a transparent cover will often turn the trick. This must be thin, however. Glass is not satisfactory, since irregularities in the surfaces will distort the reflected image. A dry-cleaning bag, sandwich bag, or plastic report cover will provide good material. Coat-hanger wire makes a convenient frame. When using a cover, you'll have to readjust the sextant filters. Even with a cover, a strong wind may affect the reflected image. This can be helped by lining your pan with wire mesh, such as window screening. Leave a small space between the mesh and the sides of the pan. In this way, ripples will have to pass through the mesh, and are dissipated in the process. You might also want to experiment with a fluid thicker than water. This seems promising, but I've had poor results with lubricating oil and mineral oil. They contain some lighter components which float to the top, causing irregularities in the surface which distort the image badly.

Once you're used to taking sun sights with the artificial horizon, you'll probably want to extend the technique to moon, planet, or star sights. This can be done, but a few differences should be noted. First of all, getting sufficient brightness is easy with the moon, and is usually no problem with planets, but may be difficult with stars. This is a case where the light-gathering properties of a telescope really help. Second, due to the changing phases of the moon, it may be necessary to use either the upper limb or the lower limb. Chapter 10 gives more material on this. Third, the corrections for the moon are different from sun corrections, and those for planets and stars are different again. The details of these corrections are given in Chapter 10. It's sufficient to say here that the apparent altitude for any of these types of sights is obtained in the same way as already shown in this chapter. Once you have the apparent altitude, the corrections for the particular body sighted are applied just as they would be with a sea-horizon sight.

5   Time

He [Worsley] still carried his sole chronometer slung around his neck. Out of the twenty-four on board the Endurance when she sailed from England, this one alone had survived.

Alfred Lansing, *Endurance*

When taking sights for finding your line of position (LOP) at sea, knowing the time is just as important as measuring the altitude. The reason for this is that LOP calculations all depend on the GP of the body sighted, and the geographic position (GP) is moving about 900 miles per hour. In other words, 4 seconds of time can make a difference of 1 mile in your LOP. Obviously, you must know the time quite exactly if your sights are to be of any use.

Before going on, let's clear up one point. I've never met the gentleman who gave the same name — minute — to both angle measurements and time measurements. He might have been a mathematician; he certainly wasn't a navigator. The double meaning of one term is a sure source of confusion, but no help is in sight for the near future. In the last chapter, the term minute referred in every case to angle measurement. In this chapter, a minute is a length of time. Courage!

In the early days of sail, knowing the time accurately was a difficult problem. Ships carried several chronometers, gimbaled against motion, protected from shocks, and carefully wound in a daily ritual. Careful comparisons were made to determine the progressive gain or loss, called the *rate*. Ships meeting at sea during a long voyage would heave to while the captains compared chronometers. In spite of all this, the time was never known with much certainty. That was an important factor in the popularity of noon sights for latitude, which are less time-dependent than most sights.

Today all this has changed. Radio receivers can pick up accurate time signals from several sources. Station WWV broadcasts time signals from Colorado and Hawaii, on frequencies of 2.5, 5, 10, 15, 20, and 25 megahertz. The Canadian time signal CHU is broadcast from Ottawa on frequencies of 3.330, 7.335, and 14.670 megahertz. These short-wave stations can be picked up almost anywhere in the world by a good receiver, and are accurate to a fraction of a second. In addition, a number of commercial broadcasting stations give time signals at certain hours. These are of the form "at the tone, the time is ten-fifteen," and are usually accurate to about a second. But when the announcer says, "It's eight-twenty, and here's the morning news," forget it. Depending on who last set the wall clock, and when, and whether the announcer's coffee is hot, he may be accurate to a second or to a minute.

Since radios are prone to breaking down at the wrong moment, and even working ones can be defeated by static, most navigators prefer to carry an accurate watch, with or without a radio. Watches are widely available with mechanisms based on tiny tuning forks, accurate within seconds per week. Also under development are watches using quartz crystals. These are capable of even better accuracy, and have displays without moving parts. They will undoubtedly supersede the tuning fork types, but the few models presently on the market have some drawbacks.

The most practical watch available to the navigator today is the tuning fork type, commonly known by the trade name Accutron. Many models are available, with prices ranging from one hundred to several hundred dollars. They all have the same type of movement inside, and all have the same basic accuracy, generally guaranteed to be within 2 seconds per day. The price difference is mostly accounted for by snappy looking cases and fancy expansion wristbands. The cheapest model will serve perfectly well. It will also have the decided advantage of coming equipped with a simple buckle-type strap, which allows the watch to lie flat. Often the next-to-cheapest model will have a date display, and this is a very useful feature. All models have sweep-second hands, which is a must. One point to check is the ease of setting the watch exactly to the second. A common arrangement, which works fine, is that pulling out the setting crown stops the watch. Set the hands a little ahead, and when the proper moment arrives, push the crown in to start the watch.

Your friendly jeweler, having sold you a watch, will be happy to set it for you. He will assure you of the accuracy of his reference, but accuracy is a relative thing. The average citizen regards 15 seconds as a negligible error, but you won't. Setting your watch to a short-wave station is best. If you don't have a set, you may have a friend who does. Failing this, your local airport's radio range may be willing to tune in WWV and hold the phone up to the speaker. This works fine, but as with any other favor, it can be overdone. Other possibilities include universities and observatories. If nothing else offers, most cities have telephone recordings of the time. These may be off by a good many seconds, but at least are readily available.

Having once set your watch, you should check it periodically. Weekly intervals are appropriate. Don't reset it each time, but keep a record of the progressive loss or gain. You'll probably find that the rate is nearly constant, and this is almost as good as having no loss or gain. Knowing when the watch was set correctly, and what its rate is, you can correct the reading to get the exact time. Neat and methodical records, kept in a small notebook with the watch, will pay dividends here.

Once you know what the rate of your watch is, you'll be tempted to take it back for adjustment. If you've been using it to take sights, you're probably getting quite accuracy-conscious. Your jeweler will adjust it for you, free of charge. Most watches can keep much better time than the guaranteed 2 seconds per day, so if yours is near that figure, adjustment is probably worthwhile. After all, it amounts to 14 seconds per week, which could put your LOP off by 3 miles.

Suppose, though, your watch has a rate of half a second per day. Naturally you'd like to get that down to a quarter second, which would amount to less than two seconds per week, or half a mile in the LOP. That's accuracy! Before you head for the store again, though, remember that the average jeweler isn't accustomed to thinking of timekeeping accuracy in these terms, and his adjustment machine isn't necessarily much better. In trying to improve on that half second per day, you may end up with a whole second, or three seconds. One or two experiences of this sort are enough to get you kicking the dog, or snarling at the kids. If your watch's rate is less than one second per day, better to leave well enough alone.

In navigating, you'll be dealing with two kinds of time. One is local time. The other is Greenwich mean time (GMT). Local time is a fancy name for the same kind of time you're already used to. It comes in 24 different varieties, or zones. This arrangement is simply one of convenience. When the sun reaches it's highest point in the sky over New York City, New Yorkers' say it's *noon*, and set their clocks to 12:00. If people in Los Angeles were to set their clocks to 12:00 at that same moment, things wouldn't work out too well, for the sun doesn't reach its high point in the Los Angeles sky for another 3 hours. By that time the Los Angeles clocks would be reading 3 P.M., and the idea of noon occurring at 3 P.M. is enough to spoil anybody's lunch. To get around this problem, the people in Los Angeles have an agreement to set their clocks 3 hours behind New York time, so that Los Angeles noon will occur at 12:00 by a Los Angeles clock. Thus New York and Los Angeles are operating with different time zones. The time zones used in North America are Atlantic (used only in Canada's Maritime Provinces), Eastern, Central, Mountain, and Pacific. The borders between zones are usually arranged to follow state or province borders, so that a given state or province will have one time zone throughout. At sea, we have no borders to consider, so time zones are arranged in segments, each one 15 degrees of longitude wide. Local is used at sea primarily for mealtimes, watch-keeping, and other routines. It also plays a part in noon latitude sights, which will be discussed in more detail in Chapter 9.

Greenwich (pronounced gren-ich) mean time (GMT) is the standard tool of the navigator. Remember, the latter uses the time to look up the GP of the sun in the Almanac, and the GP pays no heed to time zones. The GP is where it is, whether you're on Eastern time or Hong-Kong time. The Almanac, then, must use a standard time system which doesn't vary according to location. This is GMT.

Greenwich mean time is referenced to the prime meridian, or 0 degrees longitude, and is always given in the 24-hour system. Thus 9 A.M. in Greenwich is 09:00 hours GMT; 3 P.M. is 15:00 hours GMT. However, 3 P.M. in New York doesn't roll around until 5 hours later. By that time it's 8 P.M. in Greenwich, so the GMT is 20:00 hours. Although the two places have different local times, the GMT is the same in either place. At 2 P.M. in Los Angeles, it's 10 P.M. in Greenwich, and the GMT in either place is 22:00 hours. To keep the conversion straight, it's helpful to remember that the sun's GP moves around the earth from east to west, so that noon occurs in Greenwich *before* noon occurs in New York. The number of hours difference between GMT and local time for a given place is listed in the almanac.

It is possible, of course, to keep your watch set to local time, and convert to GMT for navigation purposes. This is one more thing to do, though, and affords one more place to make a mistake. In this particular case, making mistakes is easier than not making them! For this reason, it's common practice to keep navigating watches set to GMT. It's a wonderful thing to look at the watch and read GMT directly, without any conversion. GMT isn't very convenient for "housekeeping" routines on board, but this won't cause a hardship. Your navigating watch should be tucked away in a snug place anyhow, away from the hard knocks a wristwatch can get on board, and lying flat. A cheap watch or bulkhead clock set to local time will serve for shipboard routines.

A caution about dates may not go amiss here. Suppose you're cruising a few miles off the coast of Oregon, and on July 23 you take a sight of the sun at about 1 P.M. local time. Your navigating watch reads 9:15. You will realize that when it's afternoon at your location, it's a good many hours *later* at Greenwich, so the local time there must be about 9 P.M. The GMT, therefore, is 21:15. You look up the GP for this time and plot the LOP. Well and good. Later in the evening of the same day you take a star sight. Your local time is about 8 P.M., and the navigating watch reads 4:24. By the same reasoning as before, the GMT must be 04:24. You plot your LOP, and find that your position is about 30 miles back in the Oregon woods! What has happened, of course, is that while your afternoon has been slipping by, evening in Greenwich has turned to midnight and then to early morning of the next day. So when consulting your Almanac for the GP, you must use 04:24 GMT on July 24. This is the reason that a date display on your navigating watch is a very good feature.

If your location is in east longitude, similar reasoning applies, but your local time is ahead of Greenwich. For example, if you are near New Zealand, about 170 degrees east longitude, your local time is 11 hours ahead of Greenwich. A morning sight on September 17, say about 8 A.M., would be at 21:00 GMT September 16.

So far in this discussion, we've been blithely assuming that when you take a sight, you somehow automatically know what the time is according to your navigating watch. Your watch, though, is actually below decks, probably buried under a pile of clothes in some drawer or other. And taking sights from the cabin isn't really the answer.

There are two solutions to the problem. One is to have an assistant watching the time as you take the sight. At the moment you make the exact sighting, you call "Mark" — or something suitably nautical sounding — and the assistant notes the time. He can write it down, along with the angle you read off, and you can proceed to take another sight without ever moving. This is handy. The second solution is to use a stopwatch. You can write down the exact time when you start the stopwatch, and go out on deck to take your sight. At the moment of sighting, stop the stopwatch. This can be done very nicely, holding the stopwatch in the left hand as you adjust the sextant. When you go below to work out the sight, add the stopwatch reading to the time you have noted, and you have the GMT of the sight.

6   The Nautical Almanac

*I realized the mathematical truth of their motions, so well
known that astronomers compile tables of their positions
through the years and days, and the minutes of a day, with
such precision that one coming along over the sea even five
years later may, by their aid, find the standard time of any
given meridian on the earth.*

Captain Joshua Slocum, *Sailing Alone Around the World*

Once you have taken a sight and noted the time, you'll need to know
the GP. This is looked up in about half a minute in the *Nautical Almanac.*

The *Nautical Almanac* is published once a year in the United States,
Britain, and other countries. You can buy a copy at most marine supply
houses that carry charts. They'll have the current year's edition, and
usually get the coming year's edition during the summer or fall, which
is useful for someone taking off on a long cruise. The price is about $6,
and with the wealth of information contained, this has got to be one of
the best buys in books.

The Almanac has been aptly likened to a celestial bus schedule. In
some 270 pages, it gives the GP for every second of the year of the sun,
moon, 4 planets, and 173 stars. Also listed are times of the rising and
setting of the sun and moon, phases of the moon, times of civil and
nautical twilight, and times of meridian passage. The front and back inside covers have tables of sextant corrections for sun, moon, planet, and

star sights. There is a handy chart showing the positions of the planets, and other reference tables. At the back is a useful section explaining construction and the use of the tables. Consider that practically all of this data must be recalculated every year, and I think you'll agree that the book is a bargain.

Our interest at the moment is finding the sun's GP. This information is found in the daily pages, which make up the bulk of the Almanac. Each page contains data for three days, tabulated at hourly intervals. At the back of the Almanac, on tinted paper, is a "Table of Increments and Corrections." This sounds rather fearsome, but is simply a means of finding the desired values at the exact minute and second of the observation.

Before going further, I'll point out that all angles in the Almanac are given to the nearest tenth of a minute of arc. That much accuracy is fine for some applications, but it isn't necessary in marine navigation. Round off all angles to the nearest minute of arc, following the rule that 0′.5 is rounded either up or down to make an even number of minutes. Thus 23′.5 becomes 24′, and 52′.5 becomes 52′.

Until this time, we have given the position of a vessel, island, or other object in terms of latitude, measured north or south from the equator. and longitude, measured east or west from Greenwich. The GP in the Almanac, however, is expressed a little differently, and here we encounter two new terms. *Greenwich hour angle* (GHA) is somewhat equivalent to longitude, but it is measured from Greenwich *always westward* through 360 degrees. Thus, there is no need to add an E or W suffix to GHA, as there is to longitude. *Declination* (Dec) is precisely equivalent to the latitude of the GP. It is measured from the equator either north or south, and is so designated when written. The sun's declination varies from zero at the spring equinox, to about 23 degrees north at the summer solstice, back to zero at the fall equinox, then to 23 degrees south at the winter solstice, and finally back to zero at the spring equinox. This north-south shifting of the sun's GP is the cause of the earth's seasons, by the way.

The GP, then, is given in terms of GHA and Dec. Now let's find the GP of the sun on May 17, 1973, at 15h 33m 12s GMT. First turn to the right-hand daily page for May 17, reproduced in Table 2. For 17d 15h, in the "Sun" column, we find the GHA is 45°55′ and the Dec is 19°23′ N. The Dec is changing slowly from hour to hour, about 0′.6 in this case, so we take the Dec figure as final. The GHA is increasing by 15° every hour, though, so we must allow for the extra 33m 12s. Turn to

Table 2.

1973 MAY 16, 17, 18 (WED., THURS., FRI.)

G.M.T.	SUN G.H.A.	SUN Dec.	MOON G.H.A.	v	MOON Dec.	d	H.P.
16 00	180 55·5	N19 01·0	15 47·6	12·6	S19 24·7	8·1	54·6
01	195 55·5	01·6	30 19·2	12·5	19 32·8	7·9	54·6
02	210 55·5	02·2	44 50·7	12·4	19 40·7	7·9	54·6
03	225 55·5 ··	02·8	59 22·1	12·4	19 48·6	7·8	54·6
04	240 55·5	03·4	73 53·5	12·4	19 56·4	7·7	54·5
05	255 55·5	03·9	88 24·9	12·3	20 04·1	7·7	54·5
W 06	270 55·5	N19 04·5	102 56·2	12·3	S20 11·8	7·5	54·5
E 07	285 55·5	05·1	117 27·5	12·3	20 19·3	7·4	54·5
D 08	300 55·5	05·7	131 58·8	12·2	20 26·7	7·3	54·5
N 09	315 55·4 ··	06·3	146 30·0	12·2	20 34·0	7·3	54·5
E 10	330 55·4	06·8	161 01·2	12·2	20 41·3	7·1	54·5
S 11	345 55·4	07·4	175 32·4	12·1	20 48·4	7·0	54·5
D 12	0 55·4	N19 08·0	190 03·5	12·0	S20 55·4	7·0	54·4
A 13	15 55·4	08·6	204 34·5	12·1	21 02·4	6·8	54·4
Y 14	30 55·4	09·1	219 05·6	12·0	21 09·2	6·7	54·4
15	45 55·4 ··	09·7	233 36·6	12·0	21 15·9	6·7	54·4
16	60 55·4	10·3	248 07·6	11·9	21 22·6	6·5	54·4
17	75 55·4	10·8	262 38·5	11·9	21 29·1	6·5	54·4
18	90 55·3	N19 11·4	277 09·4	11·8	S21 35·6	6·3	54·4
19	105 55·3	12·0	291 40·2	11·9	21 41·9	6·2	54·4
20	120 55·3	12·6	306 11·1	11·8	21 48·1	6·1	54·4
21	135 55·3 ··	13·1	320 41·9	11·7	21 54·2	6·1	54·4
22	150 55·3	13·7	335 12·6	11·7	22 00·3	5·9	54·3
23	165 55·3	14·3	349 43·3	11·7	22 06·2	5·8	54·3
17 00	180 55·3	N19 14·8	4 14·0	11·7	S22 12·0	5·7	54·3
01	195 55·2	15·4	18 44·7	11·6	22 17·7	5·6	54·3
02	210 55·2	16·0	33 15·3	11·6	22 23·3	5·5	54·3
03	225 55·2 ··	16·5	47 45·9	11·6	22 28·8	5·4	54·3
04	240 55·2	17·1	62 16·5	11·5	22 34·2	5·3	54·3
05	255 55·2	17·7	76 47·0	11·5	22 39·5	5·2	54·3
T 06	270 55·2	N19 18·2	91 17·5	11·5	S22 44·7	5·1	54·3
H 07	285 55·2	18·8	105 48·0	11·4	22 49·8	4·9	54·3
U 08	300 55·1	19·4	120 18·4	11·5	22 54·7	4·9	54·3
R 09	315 55·1 ··	19·9	134 48·9	11·3	22 59·6	4·7	54·2
S 10	330 55·1	20·5	149 19·2	11·4	23 04·3	4·6	54·2
D 11	345 55·1	21·1	163 49·6	11·3	23 08·9	4·6	54·2
A 12	0 55·1	N19 21·6	178 19·9	11·3	S23 13·5	4·4	54·2
Y 13	15 55·1	22·2	192 50·2	11·3	23 17·9	4·3	54·2
14	30 55·0	22·7	207 20·5	11·3	23 22·2	4·2	54·2
15	45 55·0 ··	23·3	221 50·8	11·2	23 26·4	4·1	54·2
16	60 55·0	23·9	236 21·0	11·2	23 30·5	3·9	54·2
17	75 55·0	24·4	250 51·2	11·2	23 34·4	3·9	54·2
18	90 55·0	N19 25·0	265 21·4	11·2	S23 38·3	3·7	54·2
19	105 54·9	25·5	279 51·6	11·1	23 42·0	3·6	54·2
20	120 54·9	26·1	294 21·7	11·1	23 45·6	3·6	54·2
21	135 54·9 ··	26·6	308 51·8	11·1	23 49·2	3·4	54·2
22	150 54·9	27·2	323 21·9	11·1	23 52·6	3·2	54·1
23	165 54·9	27·8	337 52·0	11·1	23 55·8	3·2	54·1
18 00	180 54·8	N19 28·3	352 22·1	11·0	S23 59·0	3·1	54·1
01	195 54·8	28·9	6 52·1	11·0	24 02·1	2·9	54·1
02	210 54·8	29·4	21 22·1	11·0	24 05·0	2·9	54·1
03	225 54·8 ··	30·0	35 52·1	11·0	24 07·9	2·7	54·1
04	240 54·8	30·6	50 22·1	11·0	24 10·6	2·6	54·1
05	255 54·7	31·1	64 52·1	11·0	24 13·2	2·4	54·1
F 06	270 54·7	N19 31·6	79 22·1	10·9	S24 15·6	2·4	54·1
R 07	285 54·7	32·2	93 52·0	11·0	24 18·0	2·3	54·1
I 08	300 54·7	32·7	108 22·0	10·9	24 20·3	2·1	54·1
D 09	315 54·7 ··	33·3	122 51·9	10·9	24 22·4	2·0	54·1
A 10	330 54·6	33·8	137 21·8	10·9	24 24·4	1·9	54·1
Y 11	345 54·6	34·4	151 51·7	10·9	24 26·3	1·8	54·1
12	0 54·6	N19 34·9	166 21·6	10·9	S24 28·1	1·7	54·1
13	15 54·6	35·5	180 51·5	10·9	24 29·8	1·5	54·1
14	30 54·5	36·0	195 21·4	10·9	24 31·3	1·4	54·1
15	45 54·5 ··	36·6	209 51·3	10·8	24 32·7	1·4	54·1
16	60 54·5	37·1	224 21·1	10·9	24 34·1	1·2	54·1
17	75 54·5	37·7	238 51·0	10·8	24 35·3	1·0	54·1
18	90 54·4	N19 38·2	253 20·8	10·9	S24 36·3	1·0	54·0
19	105 54·4	38·7	267 50·7	10·9	24 37·3	0·8	54·0
20	120 54·4	39·3	282 20·6	10·8	24 38·1	0·8	54·0
21	135 54·4 ··	39·8	296 50·4	10·9	24 38·9	0·6	54·0
22	150 54·3	40·4	311 20·3	10·8	24 39·5	0·5	54·0
23	165 54·3	40·9	325 50·1	10·9	24 40·0	0·3	54·0
	S.D. 15·8	d 0·6	S.D. 14·8		14·8		14·7

Moonrise

Lat.	Twilight Naut.	Twilight Civil	Sunrise	Moonrise 16	17	18	19
N 72	□	□	□	■	■	■	■
N 70	□	□	□	■	■	■	■
68	////	////	01 37	■	■	■	■
66	////	////	02 15	22 02	■	■	■
64	////	00 54	02 42	21 22	22 52	24 03	00 03
62	////	01 44	03 02	20 55	22 14	23 18	24 00
60	////	02 13	03 18	20 34	21 47	22 48	23 32
N 58	00 49	02 36	03 32	20 16	21 27	22 26	23 11
56	01 34	02 54	03 44	20 02	21 09	22 07	22 53
54	02 01	03 08	03 54	19 49	20 55	21 52	22 38
52	02 22	03 21	04 04	19 38	20 42	21 39	22 26
50	02 39	03 32	04 12	19 28	20 31	21 27	22 14
45	03 11	03 55	04 29	19 08	20 08	21 03	21 51
N 40	03 34	04 12	04 43	18 52	19 49	20 43	21 32
35	03 53	04 27	04 55	18 38	19 34	20 27	21 16
30	04 08	04 39	05 06	18 26	19 20	20 13	21 02
20	04 32	05 00	05 23	18 05	18 58	19 49	20 38
N 10	04 50	05 16	05 39	17 47	18 38	19 29	20 18
0	05 05	05 31	05 53	17 31	18 20	19 09	19 59
S 10	05 19	05 45	06 07	17 14	18 01	18 50	19 40
20	05 32	05 58	06 22	16 57	17 42	18 30	19 20
30	05 45	06 13	06 39	16 37	17 19	18 06	18 56
35	05 51	06 21	06 49	16 25	17 06	17 52	18 43
40	05 58	06 30	07 00	16 12	16 51	17 36	18 27
45	06 05	06 41	07 13	15 56	16 33	17 17	18 07
S 50	06 13	06 53	07 29	15 36	16 11	16 53	17 44
52	06 17	06 59	07 37	15 27	16 00	16 41	17 32
54	06 21	07 05	07 45	15 17	15 48	16 28	17 19
56	06 25	07 11	07 54	15 06	15 34	16 13	17 04
58	06 30	07 19	08 05	14 52	15 18	15 55	16 46
S 60	06 35	07 27	08 17	14 37	14 59	15 34	16 24

Moonset

Lat.	Sunset	Twilight Civil	Twilight Naut.	Moonset 16	17	18	19
N 72	□	□	□	■	■	■	■
N 70	□	□	□	■	■	■	■
68	22 21	////	////	00 51	■	■	■
66	21 41	////	////	01 25	01 14	■	■
64	21 14	23 07	////	01 51	01 55	02 07	02 40
62	20 53	22 13	////	02 10	02 23	02 45	03 25
60	20 36	21 42	////	02 27	02 44	03 12	03 54
N 58	20 22	21 19	23 12	02 41	03 02	03 33	04 17
56	20 10	21 01	22 23	02 52	03 17	03 50	04 35
54	19 59	20 46	21 54	03 03	03 30	04 05	04 51
52	19 50	20 33	21 33	03 12	03 41	04 18	05 04
50	19 42	20 22	21 15	03 21	03 51	04 29	05 16
45	19 24	19 59	20 43	03 38	04 12	04 53	05 40
N 40	19 09	19 41	20 19	03 53	04 29	05 12	05 59
35	18 58	19 26	20 01	04 05	04 44	05 27	06 16
30	18 47	19 14	19 45	04 16	04 57	05 41	06 30
20	18 30	18 53	19 21	04 35	05 18	06 04	06 54
N 10	18 14	18 37	19 03	04 51	05 37	06 25	07 14
0	18 00	18 22	18 47	05 06	05 54	06 44	07 33
S 10	17 46	18 08	18 34	05 21	06 12	07 02	07 53
20	17 31	17 54	18 21	05 38	06 31	07 23	08 13
30	17 14	17 39	18 08	05 57	06 52	07 46	08 37
35	17 04	17 31	18 01	06 08	07 05	08 00	08 51
40	16 53	17 22	17 55	06 20	07 20	08 16	09 07
45	16 39	17 11	17 47	06 35	07 37	08 35	09 26
S 50	16 23	16 59	17 39	06 54	07 59	08 58	09 50
52	16 16	16 54	17 35	07 03	08 09	09 10	10 02
54	16 10	16 47	17 31	07 13	08 21	09 23	10 15
56	15 58	16 41	17 27	07 24	08 35	09 38	10 30
58	15 47	16 33	17 22	07 36	08 50	09 56	10 48
S 60	15 35	16 25	17 17	07 51	09 09	10 17	11 10

SUN / MOON

Day	SUN Eqn. of Time 00h	12h	Mer. Pass.	MOON Mer. Pass. Upper	Lower	Age	Phase
	m s	m s	h m	h m	h m		
16	03 42	03 42	11 56	23.42	11 18	14	●
17	03 41	03 40	11 56	24.32	12 07	15	
18	03 39	03 38	11 56	00 32	12 56	16	

40

Table 3.

32ᵐ   INCREMENTS AND CORRECTIONS   **33ᵐ**

32	SUN PLANETS	ARIES	MOON	v or Corrn d	v or Corrn d	v or Corrn d
s	° ′	° ′	° ′	′ ′	′ ′	′ ′
00	8 00·0	8 01·3	7 38·1	0·0 0·0	6·0 3·3	12·0 6·5
01	8 00·3	8 01·6	7 38·4	0·1 0·1	6·1 3·3	12·1 6·6
02	8 00·5	8 01·8	7 38·6	0·2 0·1	6·2 3·4	12·2 6·6
03	8 00·8	8 02·1	7 38·8	0·3 0·2	6·3 3·4	12·3 6·7
04	8 01·0	8 02·3	7 39·1	0·4 0·2	6·4 3·5	12·4 6·7
05	8 01·3	8 02·6	7 39·3	0·5 0·3	6·5 3·5	12·5 6·8
06	8 01·5	8 02·8	7 39·6	0·6 0·3	6·6 3·6	12·6 6·8
07	8 01·8	8 03·1	7 39·8	0·7 0·4	6·7 3·6	12·7 6·9
08	8 02·0	8 03·3	7 40·0	0·8 0·4	6·8 3·7	12·8 6·9
09	8 02·3	8 03·6	7 40·3	0·9 0·5	6·9 3·7	12·9 7·0
10	8 02·5	8 03·8	7 40·5	1·0 0·5	7·0 3·8	13·0 7·0
11	8 02·8	8 04·1	7 40·8	1·1 0·6	7·1 3·8	13·1 7·1
12	8 03·0	8 04·3	7 41·0	1·2 0·7	7·2 3·9	13·2 7·2
13	8 03·3	8 04·6	7 41·2	1·3 0·7	7·3 4·0	13·3 7·2
14	8 03·5	8 04·8	7 41·5	1·4 0·8	7·4 4·0	13·4 7·3
15	8 03·8	8 05·1	7 41·7	1·5 0·8	7·5 4·1	13·5 7·3
16	8 04·0	8 05·3	7 42·0	1·6 0·9	7·6 4·1	13·6 7·4
17	8 04·3	8 05·6	7 42·2	1·7 0·9	7·7 4·2	13·7 7·4
18	8 04·5	8 05·8	7 42·4	1·8 1·0	7·8 4·2	13·8 7·5
19	8 04·8	8 06·1	7 42·7	1·9 1·0	7·9 4·3	13·9 7·5
20	8 05·0	8 06·3	7 42·9	2·0 1·1	8·0 4·3	14·0 7·6
21	8 05·3	8 06·6	7 43·1	2·1 1·1	8·1 4·4	14·1 7·6
22	8 05·5	8 06·8	7 43·4	2·2 1·2	8·2 4·4	14·2 7·7
23	8 05·8	8 07·1	7 43·6	2·3 1·2	8·3 4·5	14·3 7·7
24	8 06·0	8 07·3	7 43·9	2·4 1·3	8·4 4·6	14·4 7·8
25	8 06·3	8 07·6	7 44·1	2·5 1·4	8·5 4·6	14·5 7·9
26	8 06·5	8 07·8	7 44·3	2·6 1·4	8·6 4·7	14·6 7·9
27	8 06·8	8 08·1	7 44·6	2·7 1·5	8·7 4·7	14·7 8·0
28	8 07·0	8 08·3	7 44·8	2·8 1·5	8·8 4·8	14·8 8·0
29	8 07·3	8 08·6	7 45·1	2·9 1·6	8·9 4·8	14·9 8·1
30	8 07·5	8 08·8	7 45·3	3·0 1·6	9·0 4·9	15·0 8·1
31	8 07·8	8 09·1	7 45·5	3·1 1·7	9·1 4·9	15·1 8·2
32	8 08·0	8 09·3	7 45·8	3·2 1·7	9·2 5·0	15·2 8·2
33	8 08·3	8 09·6	7 46·0	3·3 1·8	9·3 5·0	15·3 8·3
34	8 08·5	8 09·8	7 46·2	3·4 1·8	9·4 5·1	15·4 8·3
35	8 08·8	8 10·1	7 46·5	3·5 1·9	9·5 5·1	15·5 8·4
36	8 09·0	8 10·3	7 46·7	3·6 2·0	9·6 5·2	15·6 8·5
37	8 09·3	8 10·6	7 47·0	3·7 2·0	9·7 5·3	15·7 8·5
38	8 09·5	8 10·8	7 47·2	3·8 2·1	9·8 5·3	15·8 8·6
39	8 09·8	8 11·1	7 47·4	3·9 2·1	9·9 5·4	15·9 8·6
40	8 10·0	8 11·3	7 47·7	4·0 2·2	10·0 5·4	16·0 8·7
41	8 10·3	8 11·6	7 47·9	4·1 2·2	10·1 5·5	16·1 8·7
42	8 10·5	8 11·8	7 48·2	4·2 2·3	10·2 5·5	16·2 8·8
43	8 10·8	8 12·1	7 48·4	4·3 2·3	10·3 5·6	16·3 8·8
44	8 11·0	8 12·3	7 48·6	4·4 2·4	10·4 5·6	16·4 8·9
45	8 11·3	8 12·6	7 48·9	4·5 2·4	10·5 5·7	16·5 8·9
46	8 11·5	8 12·8	7 49·1	4·6 2·5	10·6 5·7	16·6 9·0
47	8 11·8	8 13·1	7 49·3	4·7 2·5	10·7 5·8	16·7 9·0
48	8 12·0	8 13·3	7 49·6	4·8 2·6	10·8 5·9	16·8 9·1
49	8 12·3	8 13·6	7 49·8	4·9 2·7	10·9 5·9	16·9 9·2
50	8 12·5	8 13·8	7 50·1	5·0 2·7	11·0 6·0	17·0 9·2
51	8 12·8	8 14·1	7 50·3	5·1 2·8	11·1 6·0	17·1 9·3
52	8 13·0	8 14·3	7 50·5	5·2 2·8	11·2 6·1	17·2 9·3
53	8 13·3	8 14·6	7 50·8	5·3 2·9	11·3 6·1	17·3 9·4
54	8 13·5	8 14·9	7 51·0	5·4 2·9	11·4 6·2	17·4 9·4
55	8 13·8	8 15·1	7 51·3	5·5 3·0	11·5 6·2	17·5 9·5
56	8 14·0	8 15·4	7 51·5	5·6 3·0	11·6 6·3	17·6 9·5
57	8 14·3	8 15·6	7 51·7	5·7 3·1	11·7 6·3	17·7 9·6
58	8 14·5	8 15·9	7 52·0	5·8 3·1	11·8 6·4	17·8 9·6
59	8 14·8	8 16·1	7 52·2	5·9 3·2	11·9 6·4	17·9 9·7
60	8 15·0	8 16·4	7 52·5	6·0 3·3	12·0 6·5	18·0 9·8

33	SUN PLANETS	ARIES	MOON	v or Corrn d	v or Corrn d	v or Corrn d
s	° ′	° ′	° ′	′ ′	′ ′	′ ′
00	8 15·0	8 16·4	7 52·5	0·0 0·0	6·0 3·4	12·0 6·7
01	8 15·3	8 16·6	7 52·7	0·1 0·1	6·1 3·4	12·1 6·8
02·	8 15·5	8 16·9	7 52·9	0·2 0·1	6·2 3·5	12·2 6·8
03	8 15·8	8 17·1	7 53·2	0·3 0·2	6·3 3·5	12·3 6·9
04	8 16·0	8 17·4	7 53·4	0·4 0·2	6·4 3·6	12·4 6·9
05	8 16·3	8 17·6	7 53·6	0·5 0·3	6·5 3·6	12·5 7·0
06	8 16·5	8 17·9	7 53·9	0·6 0·3	6·6 3·7	12·6 7·0
07	8 16·8	8 18·1	7 54·1	0·7 0·4	6·7 3·7	12·7 7·1
08	8 17·0	8 18·4	7 54·4	0·8 0·4	6·8 3·8	12·8 7·1
09	8 17·3	8 18·6	7 54·6	0·9 0·5	6·9 3·9	12·9 7·2
10	8 17·5	8 18·9	7 54·8	1·0 0·6	7·0 3·9	13·0 7·3
11	8 17·8	8 19·1	7 55·1	1·1 0·6	7·1 4·0	13·1 7·3
12	8 18·0	8 19·4	7 55·3	1·2 0·7	7·2 4·0	13·2 7·4
13	8 18·3	8 19·6	7 55·6	1·3 0·7	7·3 4·1	13·3 7·4
14	8 18·5	8 19·9	7 55·8	1·4 0·8	7·4 4·1	13·4 7·5
15	8 18·8	8 20·1	7 56·0	1·5 0·8	7·5 4·2	13·5 7·5
16	8 19·0	8 20·4	7 56·3	1·6 0·9	7·6 4·2	13·6 7·6
17	8 19·3	8 20·6	7 56·5	1·7 0·9	7·7 4·3	13·7 7·6
18	8 19·5	8 20·9	7 56·7	1·8 1·0	7·8 4·4	13·8 7·7
19	8 19·8	8 21·1	7 57·0	1·9 1·1	7·9 4·4	13·9 7·8
20	8 20·0	8 21·4	7 57·2	2·0 1·1	8·0 4·5	14·0 7·8
21	8 20·3	8 21·6	7 57·5	2·1 1·2	8·1 4·5	14·1 7·9
22	8 20·5	8 21·9	7 57·7	2·2 1·2	8·2 4·6	14·2 7·9
23	8 20·8	8 22·1	7 57·9	2·3 1·3	8·3 4·6	14·3 8·0
24	8 21·0	8 22·4	7 58·2	2·4 1·3	8·4 4·7	14·4 8·0
25	8 21·3	8 22·6	7 58·4	2·5 1·4	8·5 4·7	14·5 8·1
26	8 21·5	8 22·9	7 58·7	2·6 1·5	8·6 4·8	14·6 8·2
27	8 21·8	8 23·1	7 58·9	2·7 1·5	8·7 4·9	14·7 8·2
28	8 22·0	8 23·4	7 59·1	2·8 1·6	8·8 4·9	14·8 8·3
29	8 22·3	8 23·6	7 59·4	2·9 1·6	8·9 5·0	14·9 8·3
30	8 22·5	8 23·9	7 59·6	3·0 1·7	9·0 5·0	15·0 8·4
31	8 22·8	8 24·1	7 59·8	3·1 1·7	9·1 5·1	15·1 8·4
32	8 23·0	8 24·4	8 00·1	3·2 1·8	9·2 5·1	15·2 8·5
33	8 23·3	8 24·6	8 00·3	3·3 1·8	9·3 5·2	15·3 8·5
34	8 23·5	8 24·9	8 00·6	3·4 1·9	9·4 5·2	15·4 8·6
35	8 23·8	8 25·1	8 00·8	3·5 2·0	9·5 5·4	15·5 8·7
36	8 24·0	8 25·4	8 01·0	3·6 2·0	9·6 5·4	15·6 8·7
37	8 24·3	8 25·6	8 01·3	3·7 2·1	9·7 5·4	15·7 8·8
38	8 24·5	8 25·9	8 01·5	3·8 2·1	9·8 5·5	15·8 8·8
39	8 24·8	8 26·1	8 01·8	3·9 2·2	9·9 5·5	15·9 8·9
40	8 25·0	8 26·4	8 02·0	4·0 2·2	10·0 5·6	16·0 8·9
41	8 25·3	8 26·6	8 02·2	4·1 2·3	10·1 5·6	16·1 9·0
42	8 25·5	8 26·9	8 02·5	4·2 2·3	10·2 5·7	16·2 9·0
43	8 25·8	8 27·1	8 02·7	4·3 2·4	10·3 5·8	16·3 9·1
44	8 26·0	8 27·4	8 02·9	4·4 2·5	10·4 5·8	16·4 9·2
45	8 26·3	8 27·6	8 03·2	4·5 2·5	10·5 5·9	16·5 9·2
46	8 26·5	8 27·9	8 03·4	4·6 2·6	10·6 5·9	16·6 9·3
47	8 26·8	8 28·1	8 03·7	4·7 2·6	10·7 6·0	16·7 9·3
48	8 27·0	8 28·4	8 03·9	4·8 2·7	10·8 6·0	16·8 9·4
49	8 27·3	8 28·6	8 04·1	4·9 2·7	10·9 6·1	16·9 9·4
50	8 27·5	8 28·9	8 04·4	5·0 2·8	11·0 6·2	17·0 9·5
51	8 27·8	8 29·1	8 04·6	5·1 2·8	11·1 6·2	17·1 9·5
52	8 28·0	8 29·4	8 04·9	5·2 2·9	11·2 6·3	17·2 9·6
53	8 28·3	8 29·6	8 05·1	5·3 3·0	11·3 6·3	17·3 9·7
54	8 28·5	8 29·9	8 05·3	5·4 3·0	11·4 6·4	17·4 9·7
55	8 28·8	8 30·1	8 05·6	5·5 3·1	11·5 6·4	17·5 9·8
56	8 29·0	8 30·4	8 05·8	5·6 3·1	11·6 6·5	17·6 9·8
57	8 29·3	8 30·6	8 06·1	5·7 3·2	11·7 6·5	17·7 9·9
58	8 29·5	8 30·9	8 06·3	5·8 3·2	11·8 6·6	17·8 9·9
59	8 29·8	8 31·1	8 06·5	5·9 3·3	11·9 6·6	17·9 10·0
60	8 30·0	8 31·4	8 06·8	6·0 3·4	12·0 6·7	18·0 10·1

the tinted "Increments and Corrections" section and find the page for 33m, reproduced in Table 3, and look down the column to 12s. Across from this figure, in the Sun-Planets column, read 8°18'. This figure must be added to the GHA for 17d 15h. Your work will look like this:

	GHA	Dec
17d 15h	45°55'	19°23'N
33m 12s	+8°12'	+0'
	54°~~13'~~ 07'	19°23'N

For another example, consider a sun sight taken at 07h 32m 46s GMT on May 18, 1973. The GP of the sun will be figured as:

	GHA	Dec
18d 07h	285°55'	19°32'N
32m 46s	+8°12'	+0'
	294°07'	19°32'N

And that's all there is to that!

The daily pages also give the times of sunrise and sunset, in local time. For example, on May 17, 1973, sunrise at latitude 35°N occurs at 04:55 local time, and sunset occurs at 18:58 local time. These figures are given for the middle day of the three days on the page, and apply to a standard meridian, i.e., a longitude that is an even multiple of 15°. In the example above, the same times would apply at longitude 45°W, or longitude 105°E. If you're not located at a standard meridian, though, you must allow for the difference. The GHA moves west 15° every hour, or 1° every 4 minutes of time, as you can see by looking at the figures in the GHA column. If you're west of a standard meridian, sunrise and sunset will occur later. For example, at longitude 47°W, they will occur 8 minutes later, at 05:03 and 19:06, respectively. At longitude 98°W, which is 7° east of the nearest standard meridian, they will occur 28 minutes earlier, at 04:27 and 18:30, respectively.

At the bottom of the daily page, in the right-hand corner, the time of the meridian passage is listed. This is the time of "noon," when the sun will be due south (due north if you are in south latitudes) and at its highest altitude in the sky. Again, these times are in local time and apply to a standard meridian. The equation of time is given in the same part of the page. This figure was important to the method of calculation in use a good many years ago, but you won't have any need of it. It is simply the length of time, before or after 12:00, that the meridian passage occurs. For example, on May 16, the meridian passage occurs 3m 42s before noon. Rounded off to the nearest minute, this is 11.56, as given under "Meridian Passage."

Other information is given on the daily pages, but we'll take it up as we come to use it. For the time being, we will use the GHA and Dec tables a great deal, and the others occasionally.

Here are some practice problems. For the times listed, find the sun's GHA and Dec. The answers are to be found in the Appendix.

1. May 18, 1973   03h   32m   05s   GMT

2. May 16   19h   33m   40s

3. May 17   12h   33m   27s

4. May 16   05h   32m   16s

7   Sight Reduction Tables

It is curious how the land comes up from the sea after a passage of many days across the open water, a passage which is measured until then only upon a chart with pencilled lines calculated from much observation of the sun and other heavenly bodies, and the working of involved trigonometrical formulas simplified by tables.

Alan Villiers, *Cruise of the Conrad*

Stop and think for a minute about the basic steps of finding an LOP. They were listed in Chapter 2.

1. Measure the altitude of the sun and note the time.
2. Using the Almanac, find the GP of the sun at the time of the observation.
3. Choose an AP, and use tables to find the calculated altitude of the sun at the AP.
4. Compare the measured with the calculated altitude, and plot the LOP.

So far we have covered the first two steps. In this chapter we will go into the details of step 3.

Nobody is ever totally lost. After all, you knew where you were yesterday, or maybe last week. By keeping track of your subsequent speed and direction, you can estimate your present position. This process is called dead reckoning (DR), and is covered in detail in Chapter 9. For now, we'll just say that with careful work a DR position may be quite accurate, perhaps a matter of a few miles from your true position. Occasionally, adverse circumstances like storms may force you to make a wild guess. This is dignified with the name estimated position (EP). For the most part, though, you work with reasonably accurate DR positions.

If we know the position of two points on the earth's surface, we can calculate the distance between the points. One such pair of points is the sun's GP, which we can look up in the Almanac, and our own DR position. The calculated distance between them could be expressed in nautical miles, but is usually given as an angle, since 60 nautical miles equal one degree. As already shown in Chapter 1, subtracting this angle from $90°$ gives the altitude of the sun as seen from the DR position. Another similar calculation will tell us the direction in which the sun will be seen from the DR position.

Since we are dealing with a spherical earth and curved lines, the equations involved in these calculations are scary-looking, involving such terms as natural versine and log haversine. For many years, the navigator had no choice but to use these equations, and that's probably the reason why navigation is regarded even today as something of a black art, comprehensible only to the chosen few. This state of affairs, of course, makes the navigator look pretty smart to the novice. Navigators, being only human, aren't always anxious to dispel the myth. Neither are authors, for that matter. A recent book on navigation gives a whole page of such mathematical gems such as

$$\tan (a + b) = \frac{\tan a + \tan b}{1 - (\tan a)(\tan b)}$$

None of these is actually used in the book or anywhere else in practical navigation.

The fact is, though, that today's navigator doesn't need to do any of these calculations. He doesn't need to know a cosine from a street sign. Mathematicians have done all the work for us, and published the answers in handy books; so we need only look up the answers. These books are called <u>Sight Reduction Tables.</u> They are available from the same sources as Almanacs. You will need a set. A nice feature of these tables is that they are permanent, just as multiplication tables are permanent. Having once acquired a set (and they are surprisingly cheap), you don't need to replace them annually, like the Almanac.

They come in several different versions, each with good and bad points. One such version, in common use aboard large ships, is the classic Hydrographic Office Publication 214 (HO 214). These tables are convenient to use and highly accurate, but come in nine volumes which cost about $45 and fill a small suitcase. They aren't the answer for the sailor. A recent 6-volume publication is HO 229, serving exactly the same function as HO 214, and just as big and expensive. A single-volume version is HO 211, very small, that costs just $1. It belongs on board every boat. It's not very convenient to use, though, and so is reserved for special situations, discussed in Chapter 11. Finally, HO 249, *Sight Reduction Tables for Air Navigators,* is the publication to use. It comes in three volumes, with red, white, and blue ring bindings. Buy Volumes II and III, $4.50 each. Volume I deals with a special method for star sights only, and is not needed. Don't be put off by the title. The air navigator needs tables which are compact and easy to use. The same features are valuable to the sailor. These tables are used in the same way as the much larger versions — HO 214 and HO 229.

In theory, sight reduction tables could be prepared to cover all possible combinations of DR and GP locations to the nearest minute of angle. Such a set of tables wouldn't be especially handy, though, for it would have about 430,000 volumes. In order to reduce the bulk to practical proportions, the tables are limited to combinations of positions to the nearest degree. This limitation means that we generally don't use our DR position with the tables, but rather a nearby position chosen to fit the whole degree entries of the tables. This chosen position is not where we really think we are (i.e., the DR position), but is a temporary assumption for convenience only. Accordingly, it is called an assumed position (AP). The assumed position will always be within 45 miles of the DR position. Of course, the DR position itself may be in error by a good deal, but this won't affect the final result.

We are going to choose the AP so its location will be known. The location of the GP is known from the Almanac. From these two known points, we pick three bits of information to enter the tables. These are:

1. The latitude of the AP (aL).

2. The difference in longitudes of the AP and GP (meridian angle).

3. The declination of the GP (Dec).

See Figure 7-1.

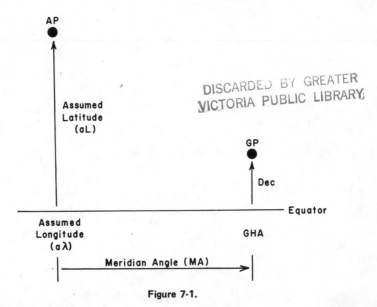

Figure 7-1.

The tables will then give us the calculated altitude of the sun (Hc) and its direction (Z), as seen from the AP. (The word *sun* is used to avoid many repetitions of "sun, moon, planets, or stars." The same tables are used in exactly the same way for any of these bodies.)

Now we're ready to choose the location of the AP. The latitude of the AP (assumed latitude or aL) will be a whole number of degrees, which-ever number is closest to our DR position. Thus, if our DR position is at 31°17′N, choose the aL to be 31°N. If the DR position is at 38°42′S, choose the aL to be 39°S.

Choose the longitude of the AP (assumed longitude or aλ). The aλ should be within 30′ of longitude of the DR position, either east or west, and the difference in longitudes of the AP and GP should be a whole number of degrees. This sounds complicated, but isn't. Consider the situation in Figure 7-2, viewed from the North Pole.

Here the GHA is 42°11′, and our DR longitude is 110°20′W. We would choose the aλ as 110°11′W, since this is less than 30′ from our DR longitude, and the angle from the AP to the GP is 68°00′ to the east. The angle from the AP to the GP is called the <u>meridian angle</u>, and may be measured either east or west, depending on whether the GP is east of the AP (rising), or west of the AP (setting). Another case is shown in Figure 7-3.

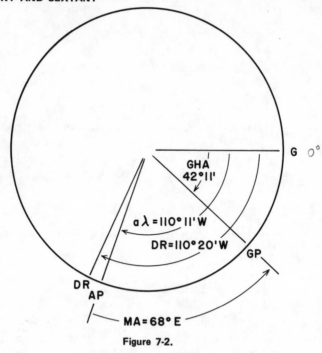

Figure 7-2.

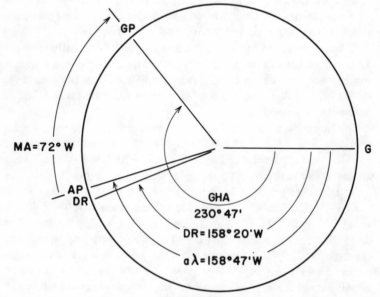

Figure 7-3.

Here the GHA is $230°47'$, and our DR longitude is $158°20'$W. We would choose an aλ of $158°47'$W, giving a meridian angle of $72°$W.

Remember that the meridian angle is <u>measured *from*</u> the AP <u>*to*</u> the GP, either east or west. In this book the meridian angle is abbreviated MA. I must explain that this angle has been given various names by different authors over the years. For a long time it was called <u>hour angle</u> (HA) by the armed forces. The HO 214 tables still list the angle under this name. However, three other angles used a great deal in navigation are the local hour angle (LHA), Greenwich hour angle (GHA), and sidereal hour angle (SHA). These angles are all measured *always west-ward*, through 360 degrees. Having another hour angle measured either east or west creates something of a conflict, so the term was gradually abandoned in favor of meridian angle. Several authors use the abbreviation "t" for this angle, for no obvious reason. To further confuse an already tangled situation, the term hour angle is still in use, but several authors fail to make the distinction between hour angle and local hour angle. Just remember that LHA, GHA, and SHA are all measured westward through 360 degrees, while the meridian angle (MA) is measured either east or west, up to 180 degrees. The names actually aren't as important as the concepts they represent.

Two more examples are in order, for cases where the AP is in east longitude. In Figure 7-4, the GHA is $160°17'$, and the DR longitude is $120°21'$E. You'll probably call the assumed longitude $120°17'$E, for a meridian angle of $40°$E. This won't work, because GHA and east longitude are measured in opposite directions. The easiest way to see the situation is to pretend for a minute that we measure from Greenwich to the GP also eastward. It's not hard to see that the angle would then be $360°00' - 160°17'$, which equals $199°43'$. We would then choose an aλ of $120°43'$E, so that the MA would be $79°$E. Another way of reasoning is that the angle from the AP ($120°43'$E) to $180°00'$ equals $59°17'$. The angle from the GP ($160°17'$) to $180°00'$ equals $19°43'$. The angle between the AP and the GP is then

$$\begin{array}{r} 59°17' \\ + \ 19°43' \\ \hline 79°00' \end{array}$$

A last example. In Figure 7-5, the GHA is $340°38'$. The DR longitude is $140°06'$E. To select the AP, consider that from Greenwich east to the GP is $360°00' - 340°38' = 19°22'$. Therefore to get an MA in whole degrees, we must pick our assumed longitude as $140°22'$E, which results in an MA of $140°22' - 19°22' = 121°00'$W.

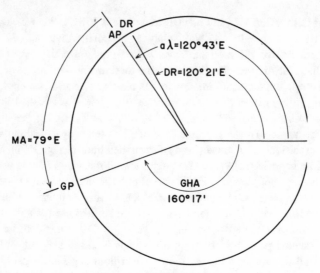

Figure 7-4.

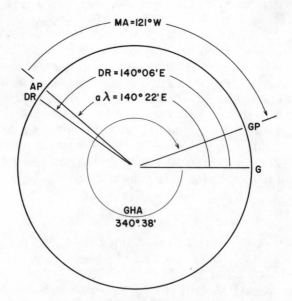

Figure 7-5.

Here's a hint. For AP's in east longitude, you'll notice that if you pick the AP correctly, the AP minutes and the GHA minutes will add up to 60', or a whole degree. Thus in Figure 7-4, 43' + 17' = 60'. In Figure 7-5, 22' + 38' = 60'.

You'll probably have to do some deep thinking about this MA business before you get used to it. Sketches are quite helpful. Fortunately, the calculation is easy when you're located in west longitude, and that's where the majority of racing and cruising is being done. I'm purposely avoiding any of the little rules that are sometimes given to do this figuring, along the lines, "If the dolittle is greater than 180, subtract it from the glofitz, add 360, and the result is the gowrong." These rules are a drag to memorize, and are forgotten (or mixed up) sooner than a cold drink disappears on a hot day. Reason through the situation, understand what you're doing, and you won't go wrong.

Here are some more practice problems. For the GP and DR position given, choose the AP and calculate the MA. Answers are to be found in the Appendix.

1. GP:	GHA	137°23'	DR position:	44°49'N
	Dec	14°07'N		53°27'W
2. GP:	GHA	310°41'	DR position:	26°33'N
	Dec	9°56'S		130°14'E
3. GP:	GHA	120°35'	DR position:	65°17'S
	Dec	22°10'S		160°07'W
4. GP:	GHA	142°38'	DR position:	32°48'N
	Dec	17°41'N		140°11'E

All right. Back a few pages, I said that we would enter the tables with

1. The latitude of the AP. You know how to choose this now — a whole degree.

2. The difference in longitudes of the AP and the GP. You know now that this is called the meridian angle, and is a whole degree because you choose the longitude of the AP to make it so.

3. The declination of the GP. Here we hit a small snag. The tables list only whole degrees of declination, but if the Dec happens to be 18°23'S, we can't change the fact. The GP is where it's at, so to

Table 4. HO 249

DECLINATION (15°-29°) SAME NAME AS LATITUDE   LAT 29°

Dec

LHA	15° Hc	d	Z	16° Hc	d	Z	17° Hc	d	Z	18° Hc	d	Z	19° Hc	d	Z	20° Hc	d	Z	21° Hc	d	Z	22° Hc	d	Z
0	76 00	+60	180	77 00	+60	180	78 00	+60	180	79 00	+60	180	80 00	+60	180	81 00	+60	180	82 00	+60	180	83 00	+60	180
1	75 58	60	176	76 58	60	176	77 58	60	175	78 58	60	175	79 58	59	175	80 57	60	174	81 57	60	173	82 57	59	172
2	75 53	59	172	76 52	60	172	77 52	59	171	78 51	59	170	79 50	59	169	80 49	59	168	81 48	58	167	82 46	58	165
3	75 44	58	168	76 43	58	167	77 41	59	166	78 40	58	165	79 38	58	164	80 36	57	163	81 33	57	161	82 30	55	158
4	75 31	58	164	76 29	58	163	77 27	57	162	78 24	57	161	79 21	57	159	80 18	55	157	81 13	55	155	82 08	52	152
5	75 16	+57	161	76 13	+56	159	77 09	+56	158	78 05	+56	156	79 01	+54	154	79 55	+54	152	80 49	+51	149	81 40	+50	146
6	74 57	56	157	75 53	55	156	76 48	54	154	77 42	54	152	78 36	53	150	79 29	51	148	80 20	49	145	81 09	47	141
7	74 35	54	154	75 29	54	152	76 23	53	150	77 16	52	148	78 08	51	146	78 59	49	143	79 48	47	140	80 35	44	136
8	74 10	54	151	75 04	52	149	75 56	51	147	76 47	50	145	77 37	49	142	78 26	47	139	79 13	44	136	79 57	41	132
9	73 43	52	147	74 35	51	146	75 26	50	144	76 16	48	141	77 04	47	139	77 51	44	136	78 35	42	133	79 17	39	129
10	73 14	+50	145	74 04	+50	143	74 54	+48	140	75 42	+46	138	76 28	+45	135	77 13	+42	133	77 55	+40	129	78 35	+37	126
11	72 42	49	142	73 31	48	140	74 19	47	138	75 06	44	135	75 50	43	133	76 33	41	130	77 14	38	126	77 52	35	123
12	72 09	47	139	72 56	47	137	73 43	45	135	74 28	43	132	75 11	41	130	75 52	39	127	76 31	36	124	77 07	33	120
13	71 34	46	137	72 20	45	135	73 05	43	132	73 48	42	130	74 30	39	127	75 09	38	124	75 47	34	121	76 21	32	118
14	70 57	45	134	71 42	43	132	72 25	42	130	73 07	40	128	73 47	38	125	74 25	36	122	75 01	33	119	75 34	30	116
15	70 18	+44	132	71 02	+42	130	71 44	+41	128	72 25	+39	125	73 04	+37	123	73 41	+34	120	74 15	+32	117	74 47	+29	114
16	69 39	42	130	70 21	41	128	71 02	40	126	71 42	37	123	72 19	36	121	72 55	33	118	73 28	30	115	73 58	28	112
17	68 58	42	128	69 40	39	126	70 19	39	124	70 58	36	122	71 34	34	119	72 08	32	116	72 40	30	114	73 10	26	111
18	68 16	41	126	68 57	38	124	69 35	37	122	70 12	36	120	70 48	33	117	71 21	31	115	71 52	28	112	72 20	26	109
19	67 34	39	125	68 13	37	123	68 50	36	120	69 26	35	118	70 01	32	116	70 33	30	113	71 03	28	111	71 31	25	108
20	66 50	+38	123	67 28	+37	121	68 05	+35	119	68 40	+33	117	69 13	+31	114	69 44	+30	112	70 14	+26	109	70 40	+25	107
21	66 05	38	121	66 43	36	119	67 19	34	117	67 53	32	115	68 25	30	113	68 55	29	111	69 24	26	108	69 50	24	106
22	65 20	37	120	65 57	35	118	66 32	33	116	67 05	31	114	67 36	30	112	68 06	28	109	68 34	25	107	68 59	23	104
23	64 34	36	119	65 10	34	117	65 44	33	115	66 17	30	113	66 47	29	110	67 16	27	108	67 43	25	106	68 08	23	103
24	63 48	35	117	64 23	33	115	64 56	32	113	65 28	30	111	65 58	28	109	66 26	27	107	66 53	24	105	67 17	22	102
25	63 01	+34	116	63 35	+33	114	64 08	+31	112	64 39	+29	110	65 08	+28	108	65 36	+26	106	66 02	+24	104	66 26	+22	102
26	62 14	33	115	62 47	32	113	63 19	30	111	63 49	29	109	64 18	27	107	64 45	26	105	65 11	23	103	65 34	22	101
27	61 26	32	114	61 58	32	112	62 30	30	110	63 00	28	108	63 28	27	106	63 55	25	104	64 20	23	102	64 43	21	100
28	60 37	33	112	61 10	30	111	61 40	30	109	62 10	27	107	62 37	25	105	63 04	24	103	63 28	23	101	63 51	21	99
29	59 49	31	111	60 20	31	110	60 51	28	108	61 19	28	106	61 47	25	104	62 12	25	102	62 37	22	100	62 59	21	98
30	59 00	+31	110	59 31	+30	109	60 01	+28	107	60 29	+27	105	60 56	+25	103	61 21	+24	102	61 45	+22	100	62 07	+20	98
31	58 10	31	109	58 41	29	108	59 10	28	106	59 38	27	104	60 05	25	103	60 30	23	101	60 53	22	99	61 15	20	97
32	57 21	30	108	57 51	29	107	58 20	27	105	58 47	26	104	59 13	25	102	59 38	23	100	60 01	22	98	60 23	20	96
33	56 31	29	108	57 00	29	106	57 29	27	104	57 56	26	103	58 22	24	101	58 46	23	99	59 09	22	97	59 31	20	96
34	55 41	29	107	56 10	28	105	56 38	27	104	57 05	25	102	57 30	24	100	57 54	23	99	58 17	21	97	58 38	20	95
35	54 50	+29	106	55 19	+28	104	55 47	+26	103	56 13	+26	101	56 39	+23	100	57 02	+22	98	57 25	+21	96	57 46	+20	94
36	54 00	28	105	54 28	28	104	54 56	26	102	55 22	25	100	55 47	23	99	56 10	23	97	56 33	21	96	56 54	19	94
37	53 09	28	104	53 37	27	103	54 04	26	101	54 30	25	100	54 55	23	98	55 18	23	97	55 41	20	95	56 01	20	93
38	52 18	28	104	52 46	27	102	53 13	25	101	53 38	25	99	54 03	23	98	54 26	22	96	54 48	21	94	55 09	19	93
39	51 27	27	103	51 54	27	101	52 21	25	100	52 46	25	98	53 11	23	97	53 34	22	95	53 56	21	94	54 17	19	92
40	50 36	+27	102	51 03	+26	101	51 29	+26	99	51 55	+24	98	52 19	+23	96	52 42	+21	95	53 03	+21	93	53 24	+19	92
41	49 44	27	101	50 11	26	100	50 37	25	99	51 02	24	97	51 26	23	96	51 49	22	94	52 11	21	93	52 32	19	91
42	48 53	27	101	49 20	25	99	49 45	25	98	50 10	24	96	50 34	23	95	50 57	22	94	51 19	20	92	51 39	19	91
43	48 01	27	100	48 28	25	99	48 53	25	97	49 18	24	96	49 42	22	95	50 05	21	93	50 26	20	92	50 47	19	90
44	47 09	27	99	47 36	25	98	48 01	25	97	48 26	24	95	48 50	22	94	49 12	22	93	49 34	20	91	49 54	20	90
45	46 17	+27	99	46 44	+25	97	47 09	+25	96	47 34	+23	95	47 57	+23	93	48 20	+21	92	48 41	+21	91	49 02	+19	89
46	45 26	26	98	45 52	25	97	46 17	24	96	46 41	24	94	47 05	22	93	47 27	22	92	47 49	20	90	48 09	20	89
47	44 34	26	98	45 00	25	96	45 25	24	95	45 49	23	94	46 12	23	92	46 35	21	91	46 56	21	90	47 17	19	88
48	43 42	25	97	44 07	25	96	44 32	25	94	44 57	23	93	45 20	22	93	45 42	22	91	46 04	20	89	46 24	20	88
49	42 49	26	96	43 15	25	95	43 40	24	94	44 04	23	93	44 27	25	91	44 50	21	90	45 11	21	89	45 32	20	87
50	41 57	+26	96	42 23	+25	95	42 48	+24	93	43 12	+23	92	43 35	+22	91	43 57	+22	90	44 19	+21	88	44 40	+19	87
51	41 05	26	95	41 31	24	94	41 55	24	93	42 19	24	92	42 43	22	90	43 05	21	89	43 26	21	88	43 47	20	86
52	40 13	25	95	40 38	25	94	41 03	24	92	41 27	23	91	41 50	22	90	42 12	22	89	42 34	21	87	42 55	20	86
53	39 20	26	94	39 46	24	93	40 10	24	92	40 34	24	91	40 58	22	89	41 20	22	88	41 42	20	87	42 02	20	86
54	38 28	25	94	38 53	25	92	39 18	24	91	39 42	23	90	40 05	23	89	40 28	21	88	40 49	21	86	41 10	20	85
55	37 36	+25	93	38 01	+25	92	38 26	+23	91	38 49	+24	90	39 13	+22	88	39 35	+22	87	39 57	+21	86	40 18	+20	85
56	36 43	25	93	37 08	25	91	37 33	24	90	37 57	23	89	38 20	23	88	38 43	22	87	39 05	21	86	39 26	20	84
57	35 51	25	92	36 16	25	91	36 41	24	90	37 05	23	89	37 28	22	88	37 50	22	86	38 12	21	85	38 33	21	84
58	34 58	26	92	35 24	24	90	35 48	24	89	36 12	23	88	36 35	23	87	36 58	22	86	37 20	21	85	37 41	21	84
59	34 06	25	91	34 31	25	90	34 56	24	89	35 20	23	88	35 43	23	87	36 06	22	85	36 28	21	84	36 49	21	83

speak. What we can do is enter the tables with the next smaller whole degree, and later make a simple correction for the difference. Now we're ready to use the tables.

Suppose you're in the North Atlantic, and your DR position is 29°15′N, 62°47′W. You take a morning sun sight on May 17, 1973, at GMT 13h 32m 08s. From the Almanac, the GP of the sun at this time is:

1973 May	GHA	Dec
17d 13h	*15°55′*	*19°22′N*
32m 08s	*+8°02′*	*+0′*
	23°57′ W	*19°22′N*

The AP is chosen as 29°N, 62°57′W. The MA is 39°E. The tables are entered with

> Lat   29°N
> Dec   19°N
> MA   39°E

Volume II covers latitudes 0° to 39°. Turn to page 177, extracted in Table 4. The page heading is "Declination *Same* Name as Latitude." This covers the case at hand, since both the Dec and the AP are north latitude. Find the Dec of 19° at the top of the page. The left-hand and right-hand columns are headed L.H.A. We are working with MA instead, since it is easier to visualize and saves a couple of steps of arithmetic. The L.H.A. and MA are numerically the same for angles less than 180°, so simply ignore the right-hand column, and read the left-hand one as MA. In the Dec 19° column, on the MA (L.H.A.) 39° line, read the values Hc = 53°11′, d = +23′, and Z = 97°.

The term Hc (i.e., height, computed) is the computed altitude, that would be observed at the AP if the sun's Dec was exactly 19°N. Since the sun's Dec is more than 19°N, we must allow for the difference, and this is where the "d" figure is used. Notice that for a Dec of 20° and the same MA of 39°, the Hc is 53°34′, or 23 minutes *more* than the Hc we have in the Dec 19° column. Hence the figure d (difference), +23′. We must simply proportion the d value, according to how much the actual Dec exceeds the entering Dec. A handy table at the back of the book and also on a loose insert) does this for us. (If you're handy with a slide rule, you may prefer to use it to solve the proportion in one setting). Table 5 shows d values across the top, and minutes of Dec difference

Table 5. HO 249

Correction to Tabulated Altitude for Minutes of Declination

′ \ d	1	2	3	19	20	21	22	23	24	25	26	27	28	29	30	31	32	33	34	35	36	37	38	39	40	41	42	43	44	45	46	47	48	49	50	51
0	0	0	0	0	0	0	0	0	0	0	0	0	0	0	0	0	0	0	0	0	0	0	0	0	0	0	0	0	0	0	0	0	0	0	0	0
1	0	0	0	0	0	0	0	0	0	0	0	0	0	0	1	1	1	1	1	1	1	1	1	1	1	1	1	1	1	1	1	1	1	1	1	1
2	0	0	0	1	1	1	1	1	1	1	1	1	1	1	1	1	1	1	1	1	1	1	1	1	1	1	1	1	1	2	2	2	2	2	2	2
3	0	0	0	1	1	1	1	1	1	1	1	1	1	1	2	2	2	2	2	2	2	2	2	2	2	2	2	2	2	2	2	2	2	2	3	3
4	0	0	0	1	1	1	1	2	2	2	2	2	2	2	2	2	2	2	2	2	2	2	3	3	3	3	3	3	3	3	3	3	3	3	3	3
5	0	0	0	2	2	2	2	2	2	2	2	2	2	2	3	3	3	3	3	3	3	3	3	3	3	3	4	4	4	4	4	4	4	4	4	4
6	0	0	0	2	2	2	2	2	2	3	3	3	3	3	3	3	3	3	3	4	4	4	4	4	4	4	4	4	4	5	5	5	5	5	5	5
7	0	0	0	2	2	2	3	3	3	3	3	3	3	3	4	4	4	4	4	4	4	4	4	5	5	5	5	5	5	5	5	5	6	6	6	6
8	0	0	0	3	3	3	3	3	3	3	3	4	4	4	4	4	4	4	5	5	5	5	5	5	5	5	6	6	6	6	6	6	6	7	7	7
9	0	0	0	3	3	3	3	3	4	4	4	4	4	4	5	5	5	5	5	5	5	6	6	6	6	6	6	6	7	7	7	7	7	7	8	8
10	0	0	1	3	3	4	4	4	4	4	4	5	5	5	5	5	5	6	6	6	6	6	6	7	7	7	7	7	7	8	8	8	8	8	8	9
11	0	0	1	3	4	4	4	4	4	5	5	5	5	5	6	6	6	6	6	6	7	7	7	7	7	8	8	8	8	8	8	9	9	9	9	9
12	0	0	1	4	4	4	4	5	5	5	5	5	6	6	6	6	6	7	7	7	7	7	8	8	8	8	8	9	9	9	9	9	10	10	10	10
13	0	0	1	4	4	5	5	5	5	5	6	6	6	6	7	7	7	7	7	8	8	8	8	8	9	9	9	9	10	10	10	10	10	11	11	11
14	0	0	1	4	5	5	5	5	6	6	6	6	7	7	7	7	7	8	8	8	8	9	9	9	9	10	10	10	10	11	11	11	11	11	12	12
15	0	1	1	5	5	5	6	6	6	6	7	7	7	7	8	8	8	8	9	9	9	9	10	10	10	10	11	11	11	11	12	12	12	12	13	13
16	0	1	1	5	5	6	6	6	6	7	7	7	7	8	8	8	9	9	9	9	10	10	10	10	11	11	11	11	12	12	12	13	13	13	13	14
17	0	1	1	5	6	6	6	7	7	7	7	8	8	8	9	9	9	9	10	10	10	10	11	11	11	12	12	12	12	13	13	13	14	14	14	14
18	0	1	1	6	6	6	7	7	7	8	8	8	8	9	9	9	10	10	10	11	11	11	11	12	12	12	13	13	13	14	14	14	14	15	15	15
19	0	1	1	6	6	7	7	7	8	8	8	9	9	9	10	10	10	10	11	11	11	12	12	12	13	13	13	14	14	14	15	15	15	16	16	16
20	0	1	1	6	7	7	7	8	8	8	9	9	9	10	10	10	11	11	11	12	12	12	13	13	13	14	14	14	15	15	15	16	16	16	17	17
21	0	1	1	7	7	7	8	8	8	9	9	9	10	10	11	11	11	12	12	12	13	13	13	14	14	14	15	15	15	16	16	16	17	17	18	18
22	0	1	1	7	7	8	8	8	9	9	10	10	10	11	11	11	12	12	12	13	13	14	14	14	15	15	15	16	16	17	17	17	18	18	18	19
23	0	1	1	7	8	8	8	9	9	10	10	10	11	11	12	12	12	13	13	13	14	14	15	15	15	16	16	16	17	17	18	18	18	19	19	20
24	0	1	1	8	8	8	9	9	10	10	10	11	11	12	12	12	13	13	14	14	14	15	15	16	16	16	17	17	18	18	18	19	19	20	20	20
25	0	1	1	8	8	9	9	10	10	10	11	11	12	12	13	13	13	14	14	15	15	15	16	16	17	17	18	18	18	19	19	20	20	20	21	21
26	0	1	1	8	9	9	10	10	10	11	11	12	12	13	13	13	14	14	15	15	16	16	16	17	17	18	18	19	19	20	20	20	21	21	22	22
27	0	1	1	9	9	9	10	10	11	11	12	12	13	13	14	14	14	15	15	16	16	17	17	18	18	18	19	19	20	20	21	21	22	22	23	23
28	0	1	1	9	9	10	10	11	11	12	12	13	13	14	14	14	15	15	16	16	17	17	18	18	19	19	20	20	21	21	21	22	22	23	23	24
29	0	1	1	9	10	10	11	11	12	12	13	13	14	14	15	15	15	16	16	17	17	18	18	19	19	20	20	21	21	22	22	23	23	24	24	25
30	1	1	2	10	10	11	11	12	12	13	13	14	14	15	15	16	16	17	17	18	18	19	19	20	20	21	21	22	22	23	23	24	24	25	25	26
31	1	1	2	10	10	11	11	12	12	13	13	14	14	15	16	16	17	17	18	18	19	19	20	20	21	21	22	22	23	23	24	24	25	25	26	26
32	1	1	2	10	11	11	12	12	13	13	14	14	15	15	16	17	17	18	18	19	19	20	20	21	21	22	22	23	23	24	25	25	26	26	27	27
33	1	1	2	10	11	12	12	13	13	14	14	15	15	16	17	17	18	18	19	19	20	20	21	21	22	23	23	24	24	25	25	26	26	27	28	28
34	1	1	2	11	11	12	12	13	14	14	15	15	16	16	17	18	18	19	19	20	20	21	22	22	23	23	24	24	25	26	26	27	27	28	28	29
35	1	1	2	11	12	12	13	13	14	15	15	16	16	17	18	18	19	19	20	20	21	22	22	23	23	24	25	25	26	26	27	27	28	29	29	30
36	1	1	2	11	12	13	13	14	14	15	16	16	17	17	18	19	19	20	20	21	22	22	23	23	24	25	25	26	26	27	28	28	29	29	30	31
37	1	1	2	12	12	13	14	14	15	15	16	17	17	18	19	19	20	20	21	22	22	23	23	24	25	25	26	27	27	28	28	29	30	30	31	31
38	1	1	2	12	13	13	14	15	15	16	16	17	18	18	19	20	20	21	22	22	23	23	24	25	25	26	27	27	28	29	29	30	30	31	32	32
39	1	1	2	12	13	14	14	15	16	16	17	18	18	19	20	20	21	21	22	23	23	24	25	25	26	27	27	28	29	29	30	31	31	32	33	33
40	1	1	2	13	13	14	15	15	16	17	17	18	19	19	20	21	21	22	23	23	24	25	25	26	27	27	28	29	29	30	31	31	32	33	33	34
41	1	1	2	13	14	14	15	16	16	17	18	18	19	20	21	21	22	23	23	24	25	25	26	27	27	28	29	29	30	31	31	32	33	33	34	35
42	1	1	2	13	14	15	15	16	17	18	18	19	20	20	21	22	22	23	24	25	25	26	27	27	28	29	29	30	31	32	32	33	34	34	35	36
43	1	1	2	14	14	15	16	16	17	18	19	19	20	21	22	22	23	24	24	25	26	27	27	28	29	29	30	31	32	32	33	34	34	35	36	37
44	1	1	2	14	15	15	16	17	18	18	19	20	21	21	22	23	23	24	25	26	26	27	28	29	29	30	31	32	32	33	34	34	35	36	37	37
45	1	2	2	14	15	16	17	17	18	19	20	20	21	22	23	23	24	25	26	26	27	28	29	29	30	31	32	32	33	34	35	35	36	37	38	38
46	1	2	2	15	15	16	17	18	18	19	20	21	21	22	23	24	25	25	26	27	28	28	29	30	31	31	32	33	34	35	35	36	37	38	38	39
47	1	2	2	15	16	16	17	18	19	20	20	21	22	23	24	24	25	26	27	27	28	29	30	31	31	32	33	34	34	35	36	37	38	38	39	40
48	1	2	2	15	16	17	18	18	19	20	21	22	22	23	24	25	26	26	27	28	29	30	30	31	32	33	34	34	35	36	37	38	38	39	40	41
49	1	2	2	16	16	17	18	19	20	20	21	22	23	24	25	25	26	27	28	29	29	30	31	32	33	33	34	35	36	37	38	38	39	40	41	42
50	1	2	2	16	17	18	18	19	20	21	22	23	23	24	25	26	27	28	28	29	30	31	32	33	33	34	35	36	37	38	38	39	40	41	42	43
51	1	2	3	16	17	18	19	20	20	21	22	23	24	25	26	26	27	28	29	30	31	31	32	33	34	35	36	37	37	38	39	40	41	42	43	43
52	1	2	3	16	17	18	19	20	21	22	23	23	24	25	26	27	28	29	29	30	31	32	33	34	35	36	36	37	38	39	40	41	42	42	43	44
53	1	2	3	17	18	19	19	20	21	22	23	24	25	26	27	27	28	29	30	31	32	33	34	34	35	36	37	38	39	40	41	42	42	43	44	45
54	1	2	3	17	18	19	20	21	22	23	23	24	25	26	27	28	29	30	31	32	32	33	34	35	36	37	38	39	40	41	41	42	43	44	45	46
55	1	2	3	17	18	19	20	21	22	23	24	25	26	27	28	28	29	30	31	32	33	34	35	36	37	38	39	39	40	41	42	43	44	45	46	47
56	1	2	3	18	19	20	21	21	22	23	24	25	26	27	28	29	30	31	32	33	34	35	35	36	37	38	39	40	41	42	43	44	45	46	47	48
57	1	2	3	18	19	20	21	22	23	24	25	26	27	28	29	29	30	31	32	33	34	35	36	37	38	39	40	41	42	43	44	45	46	47	48	48
58	1	2	3	18	19	20	21	22	23	24	25	26	27	28	29	30	31	32	33	34	35	36	37	38	39	40	41	42	43	44	44	45	46	47	48	49
59	1	2	3	19	20	21	22	23	24	25	26	27	28	29	30	30	31	32	33	34	35	36	37	38	39	40	41	42	43	44	45	46	47	48	49	50

down the side. Enter the table with 23′ and 22′, respectively, and read the number 8. This is the number of minutes correction to the tabulated Hc, and must be added, since the *d* value was (+). The corrected Hc, then, is 53°19′. This is the computed altitude for the AP and the actual declination of the sun.

The figure in the *Z* column is the azimuth angle, given in whole degrees. This impressive sounding name simply gives us the bearing, or direction, of the sun from the AP. Notice that the maximum value of *Z* is 180 degrees. Since a whole circle contains 360 degrees, we have to specify which part of the circle we are dealing with. This is done simply by writing down the *Z* number with an *N* prefix, since the AP is in north latitude, and an *E* suffix, since the meridian angle is east. Thus we write N97E. The worksheet for the sight would look like this:

	GHA	Dec
17d 13h	15°55′	19°22′N
32m 08s	+8°02′	+0′
	23°57′	19°22′N
aλ	62°57′W	Tab Dec 19° Same
MA	39°E	Tab Hc = 53°11′ d = +23′ Z = N97°E
aL	19°N	cor +08′
		Hc = 53°19′

This completes step 3 of the 4 steps in plotting the LOP, since we have now chosen an AP and found the Hc and bearing (*Z*) of the sun. Before going on to step 4, though, a couple of notes are in order.

First of all, note that each page of the tables gives rules for converting the azimuth angle (*Z*) into azimuth (*Zn*). For the record, azimuth is also the bearing of the sun, but is measured always from north, clockwise through 360 degrees. By working with *Z* directly, we eliminate this conversion step, and eliminate another step later when we plot the LOP. The *Z* expression of N97E just means that we measure the sun's bearing from north, 97 degrees in an easterly direction. More on this in the next chapter.

Second, the arrangement of the worksheet shown is no accident, and I suggest that you follow it until such time as you develop your own. The GHA and Dec figuring is arranged in the same order that the Almanac is entered. The GHA and aλ are adjacent, for easy calculation of the MA. The aλ and aL are close to each other, which is handy when plotting the AP. The tabulated declination, with which the tables are entered, is adjacent to the actual declination for easy comparison when finding the Hc correction. Finally, one line lists MA, Hc, d, and Z, in the same order as they appear on one line in the table. Now for a few more examples.

In the North Pacific, at DR position 28°43′N, 121°18′W, a navigator takes an early afternoon sun sight at GMT 21h 32m 11s on May 16, 1973. The work is shown below.

	GHA	Dec		
16d 21h	135°55′	19°13′N		
32m 11s	+8°03′	+0′		
	143°58′	19°13′N		
aλ	120°58′W	Tab Dec 19° Same		
MA	23°W	Tab Hc = 66°47′	d = +29′	Z = N110°W
aL	29°N	cor	+06′	
		Hc = 66°53′		

Note here that aλ is 120°58′, which is only 20 minutes of arc from the DR longitude, rather than 121°58′, which is 40 minutes of arc from the DR longitude. Also note that the Hc correction is again added, since d is (+).

Another example: in the South Atlantic, not far off Africa, a navigator takes an afternoon sun sight on May 17, 1973, at GMT 15h 33m 47s. The DR position is 28°37′S, 12°04′E.

	GHA	Dec		
17d 15h	45°55′	19°23′N		
33m 47s	+8°27′	+0′		
	54°22′	19°23′N		
aλ	11°38′E	Tab Dec 19° Contrary		
MA	66°W	Tab Hc = 10°17′	d = -35′	Z = S119°W
aL	29°S	cor	-13′	
		Hc = 10°04′		

In this example, the meridian angle wants careful thinking, since the aλ is in east longitude. The figure of 66°W makes sense, though, since we know that in the afternoon the sun is in the west. The tables are entered for latitude 29°, declination *contrary* to latitude, since the AP is in south latitude and the Dec is north (see Table 6). The correction to the tabulated Hc is subtracted, since d is (-). The azimuth angle *(Z)* is

Table 6. HO 249

LHA	15° Hc	d	Z	16° Hc	d	Z	17° Hc	d	Z	18° Hc	d	Z	19° Hc	d	Z	20° Hc	d	Z	21° Hc	d	Z	22° Hc	d	Z
69	1013	34	114	0939	34	115	0905	33	115	0832	34	116	0758	34	117	0724	34	118	0650	34	119	0616	35	119
68	1101	34	115	1027	34	115	0953	34	116	0919	35	117	0844	34	118	0810	34	118	0736	35	119	0701	35	120
67	1148	35	115	1114	34	116	1040	35	116	1005	34	117	0931	35	118	0856	35	119	0821	35	120	0746	35	121
66	1236	34	115	1202	35	116	1127	35	117	1052	35	118	(1017	35	118)	0942	35	119	0907	36	120	0831	35	121
65	1323	-34	116	1249	-36	117	1213	-35	118	1138	-35	118	1103	-35	119	1028	-36	120	0952	-36	121	0916	-35	122
64	1410	35	116	1335	35	117	1300	36	118	1224	35	119	1149	36	120	1113	36	121	1037	36	121	1001	36	122
63	1457	35	117	1422	36	118	1346	36	119	1310	36	120	1234	36	120	1158	36	121	1122	37	122	1045	36	123
62	1544	36	118	1508	36	119	1432	36	119	1356	37	120	1319	36	121	1243	37	122	1206	37	123	1129	37	123
61	1630	36	118	1554	36	119	1518	37	120	1441	37	121	1404	37	122	1327	37	123	1250	37	123	1213	38	124
60	1716	36	119	1640	-37	120	1603	-37	121	1526	-37	121	1449	38	122	1411	-37	123	1334	-38	124	1256	-38	125
59	1802	37	120	1725	37	120	1648	37	121	1611	38	122	1533	38	123	1455	38	124	1417	38	124	1339	38	125
58	1848	38	120	1810	37	121	1733	39	122	1655	38	123	1617	38	123	1539	38	124	1501	39	125	1422	39	126
57	1933	38	121	1855	38	122	1817	38	122	1739	38	123	1701	39	124	1622	39	125	1543	39	126	1504	39	126
56	2018	38	121	1940	-39	122	1901	38	123	1823	39	124	1744	39	125	1705	39	125	1626	39	126	1547	40	127
55	2103	39	122	2024	-39	123	1945	-39	124	1906	-39	125	1827	-39	125	1748	40	127	1708	40	127	1628	40	128
54	2147	39	123	2108	39	124	2029	40	124	1949	39	125	1910	40	126	1830	40	127	1750	40	128	1710	41	128
53	2231	39	123	2152	40	124	2112	40	125	2032	40	126	1952	40	127	1912	41	127	1831	40	128	1751	41	129
52	2315	40	124	2235	40	125	2155	40	126	2115	41	127	2034	41	127	1953	41	129	1912	41	129	1831	41	130
51	2358	40	125	2318	41	126	2237	40	126	2157	41	127	2116	42	128	2034	41	129	1953	41	130	1912	42	130
50	2441	41	126	2400	41	126	2319	41	127	2238	41	128	2157	42	129	2115	42	129	2033	42	131	1951	42	131
49	2523	41	126	2442	41	127	2401	42	128	2319	41	129	2238	42	129	2156	43	130	2113	42	131	2031	43	132
48	2606	42	127	2524	42	128	2442	42	129	2400	42	129	2318	43	130	2235	42	131	2153	43	132	2110	43	132
47	2647	42	128	2605	42	129	2523	42	129	2441	43	130	2358	43	131	2315	43	132	2232	44	132	2148	43	133
46	2729	43	128	2646	43	129	2603	42	130	2521	44	131	2437	43	132	2354	44	132	2310	44	133	2226	44	134
45	2810	43	129	2727	44	130	2643	43	131	2600	44	132	2516	44	132	2432	44	133	2348	44	134	2304	44	135
44	2850	43	130	2807	44	131	2723	44	132	2639	44	132	2555	44	133	2511	45	134	2426	45	135	2341	45	135
43	2930	44	131	2846	44	132	2802	44	132	2718	45	133	2633	45	134	2548	45	135	2503	45	135	2418	46	136
42	3009	44	132	2925	45	132	2840	44	133	2756	45	134	2711	46	135	2625	45	135	2540	46	136	2454	46	137
41	3048	44	133	3004	46	133	2918	45	134	2833	45	135	2748	46	136	2702	46	136	2616	46	137	2530	47	138
40	3127	45	133	3042	46	134	2956	45	135	2910	46	136	2824	46	136	2738	47	137	2651	46	138	2605	47	138
39	3205	46	134	3119	46	135	3033	46	136	2947	46	136	2900	47	137	2813	47	138	2726	47	139	2639	47	139
38	3242	46	135	3156	47	136	3109	46	137	3023	47	137	2936	48	138	2848	47	139	2801	48	139	2713	48	140
37	3319	47	136	3232	47	137	3145	47	138	3058	48	138	3010	47	139	2923	48	140	2835	48	140	2747	49	141
36	3355	47	137	3308	48	138	3220	47	138	3133	48	139	3045	49	140	2956	48	140	2908	49	141	2819	48	142
35	3431	48	138	3343	48	139	3255	48	139	3207	49	140	3118	48	141	3030	49	141	2941	49	142	2852	50	143
34	3506	49	139	3417	48	139	3329	49	140	3240	49	141	3151	49	142	3102	49	142	3013	50	143	2923	50	144
33	3540	49	140	3451	49	140	3402	49	141	3313	49	142	3224	50	142	3134	50	143	3044	50	144	2954	50	144
32	3614	50	141	3524	49	141	3435	50	142	3345	50	143	3255	50	143	3205	50	144	3115	51	145	3024	50	145
31	3647	50	142	3557	50	142	3507	50	143	3417	51	144	3326	50	144	3236	51	145	3145	51	146	3054	51	146
30	3719	50	143	3629	51	143	3538	51	144	3447	50	145	3357	52	145	3305	51	146	3214	51	147	3123	52	147
29	3750	50	144	3700	51	144	3609	52	145	3517	51	146	3426	52	146	3334	51	147	3243	52	148	3151	52	148
28	3821	51	145	3730	52	145	3638	51	146	3547	52	147	3455	52	147	3403	52	148	3311	53	148	3218	52	149
27	3851	52	146	3759	52	146	3707	52	147	3615	52	148	3523	53	148	3430	52	149	3338	53	149	3245	53	150
26	3920	52	147	3828	53	147	3735	52	148	3643	53	149	3550	53	149	3457	53	150	3404	53	150	3311	55	151
25	3948	52	148	3856	53	149	3803	53	149	3710	53	150	3617	54	150	3523	53	151	3430	54	151	3336	54	152
24	4016	53	149	3923	54	150	3829	53	150	3736	54	151	3642	54	151	3548	54	152	3454	54	152	3400	54	153
23	4042	53	150	3949	54	151	3855	54	151	3801	54	152	3707	54	152	3613	55	153	3518	54	154	3424	55	155
22	4108	54	151	4014	54	152	3920	55	152	3825	54	153	3731	55	154	3636	55	154	3541	55	155	3446	55	155
21	4133	55	153	4038	54	153	3944	55	154	3849	55	154	3754	55	155	3659	55	156	3603	55	156	3508	56	156
20	4157	55	154	4102	56	154	4006	55	155	3911	55	155	3816	56	156	3720	55	156	3625	56	157	3529	56	157
19	4219	55	155	4124	55	155	4028	55	156	3933	56	156	3837	56	157	3741	56	157	3645	56	158	3549	56	158
18	4241	56	156	4145	56	157	4049	56	157	3953	56	158	3857	56	158	3801	57	158	3704	56	159	3608	57	159
17	4302	56	157	4206	57	158	4109	56	158	4013	57	159	3916	56	159	3820	57	160	3723	57	160	3626	57	160
16	4322	57	159	4225	57	159	4128	56	159	4032	57	160	3935	57	160	3838	58	161	3740	57	161	3643	57	161
15	4340	57	160	4243	57	161	4146	57	161	4049	57	161	3952	58	161	3854	57	162	3757	57	162	3700	58	163
14	4358	57	161	4301	58	162	4203	57	162	4106	58	162	4008	58	163	3910	57	163	3813	58	163	3715	58	164
13	4415	58	162	4317	58	163	4219	58	163	4121	58	163	4023	58	164	3925	58	164	3827	58	164	3729	58	165
12	4430	58	164	4332	58	164	4234	58	164	4136	58	165	4037	58	165	3939	58	165	3841	58	166	3742	58	166
11	4444	58	165	4346	59	165	4247	58	166	4149	59	166	4050	58	166	3952	59	167	3853	58	167	3755	59	167
10	4457	58	166	4359	59	167	4300	59	167	4201	59	167	4102	58	167	4004	59	168	3905	59	168	3806	59	168
9	4509	59	168	4410	59	168	4311	59	168	4212	59	168	4113	59	169	4014	59	169	3915	59	169	3816	59	169
8	4520	60	169	4420	59	169	4321	59	170	4222	59	170	4123	59	170	4024	59	170	3925	60	170	3825	59	171
7	4529	59	170	4430	60	171	4330	59	171	4231	59	171	4132	60	171	4032	59	171	3933	60	172	3833	59	172
6	4537	59	172	4438	60	172	4338	59	172	4239	60	172	4139	59	172	4040	60	173	3940	60	173	3840	60	173
5	4544	59	173	4445	60	173	4345	60	173	4245	59	174	4146	60	174	4046	60	174	3946	60	174	3846	59	174
4	4550	60	175	4450	60	175	4350	59	175	4251	60	175	4151	60	175	4051	60	175	3951	60	175	3851	59	175
3	4554	60	176	4454	59	176	4355	60	176	4255	60	176	4155	60	176	4055	60	176	3955	60	176	3855	60	176
2	4558	60	177	4458	60	177	4358	60	177	4258	60	177	4158	60	178	4058	60	178	3958	60	178	3858	60	178
1	4559	60	179	4459	60	179	4359	59	179	4259	60	179	4159	60	179	4059	59	179	3959	59	179	3900	60	179
0	4600	60	180	4500	60	180	4400	60	180	4300	60	180	4200	60	180	4100	60	180	4000	60	180	3900	60	180

| | 15° | 16° | 17° | 18° | 19° | 20° | 21° | 22° | Dec |

DECLINATION (15°–29°) CONTRARY NAME TO LATITUDE   LAT 29°

prefixed by S, since the AP is in south latitude, and suffixed by W, since the meridian angle is west. Finally, it's interesting to note that the sun is rather far west (66°) of the AP, and consequently quite low in the sky (10°04').

OK. We've now seen how to use the tables to obtain the calculated altitude (Hc) and the azimuth angle (Z) for the assumed position. The remaining step is to plot the LOP. This is very simply done, as shown in Chapter 8.

Here are some further practice problems. Answers to be found in the Appendix. Find the values of Hc and Z:

5. DR L: 29°24'S   6. DR L: 28°32'N
   Dec: 19°17'S   Dec: 15°07'S
   MA: 14°E   MA: 53°W

7. DR L: 29°17'N   8. DR L: 28°45'S
   Dec: 21°48'N   Dec: 18°37'N
   MA: 31°W   MA: 48°E

8 Plotting the Line of Position

> *Then the position report came. We were at 40°17'N and 63°7'W. That was great news! It showed that my navigation was reasonably accurate, for the position I had calculated was less than six miles from that given by the Columbia's navigator.*
>
> Robert Manry, *Tinkerbelle*

Once you've chosen an AP, and looked up the calculated altitude (Hc) and bearing (Z) of the sun at the AP, you're ready to plot the LOP. As outlined in Chapter 3, the plot is made by starting at the AP, measuring toward or away from the sun a distance obtained by comparing the calculated altitude (Hc) with the observed altitude (Ho), and drawing the LOP as a perpendicular.

In all plotting practice, and in much of the actual plotting done at sea, it is convenient to use plotting sheets, rather than the actual chart. This saves defacing the chart with a confusion of lines and erasures. Each sight, or set of sights, can be plotted on a separate sheet. Practice sights can thus be saved for reference, and it's rather satisfying to accumulate a growing pile of increasingly accurate sights. At sea, only the actual fix need be transferred to the chart. All the examples in this book are given in plotting-sheet form. The method of constructing plotting sheets is given at the end of Chapter 9.

Start by plotting the AP. It will be at a whole degree of latitude, which is convenient. Use dividers to locate the correct longitude. The

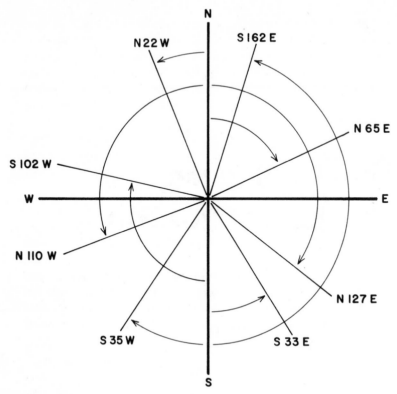

Figure 8-1.

point should be labeled AP. Next, draw a light line from the AP in the direction of the sun's bearing (Z). This is conveniently done by placing a protractor so that the center mark and the 90° mark are lined up on the latitude line, and measuring from the top or bottom index, according to whether Z is prefixed with N or S. Figure 8-1 shows some examples of the method. A protractor with scales running in both directions is helpful.

Next, calculate the difference between Hc and Ho, often called the "intercept". This will be less than 1 degree, so is simply written as a figure representing the number of minutes of arc difference, with the label *a* to identify it. I've never discovered that *a* stands for anything particular, but it's use is nearly universal. The *a* value is suffixed with T or A, according to whether the LOP is toward the sun (Ho greater than Hc) or away from the sun (Hc greater than Ho). The reasoning behind the toward or away choice derives from Chapter 3. As we move toward the sun's GP, the observed altitude increases. Accordingly, if we move from the AP toward the sun, the observed altitude (Ho) will be greater than the altitude (Hc) at the AP. One of the easiest ways to keep the A-T choice straight is given by Dutton. Remember the names Coast Guard Academy (for *C*omputed *G*reater, *A*way) and HoMoTo (for *Ho More, T*oward). A few examples will illustrate the method of calculating and labeling a.

Hc	=	32°48′	Ho	=	67°33′	Hc	=	45°06′
Ho	=	32°39′	Hc	=	67°12′	Ho	=	44°51′
a	=	09A	a	=	21T	a	=	15A

Finally, remember that one minute of arc equals one nautical mile. Accordingly, the value of a gives the number of miles to measure from the AP, in the direction Z, to plot the perpendicular LOP. For example, suppose a sun sight gives an observed altitude (Ho) of 29°46′. For the chosen AP, the tables show Hc = 29°34′ and Z = N127E. The value of a is then 12T, and the LOP is plotted as shown in Figure 8-2. The dividers are used to measure 12′ on the latitude scale, which equals 12 miles, and transfer this to the Z line. To draw the perpendicular LOP, the protractor is most convenient. This sight, incidentally, would be in mid-morning, with the sun bearing southeast.

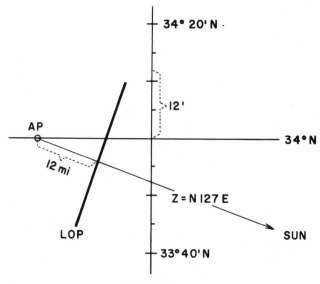

Figure 8-2.

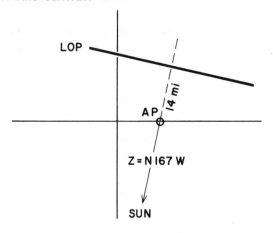

Figure 8-3(a).

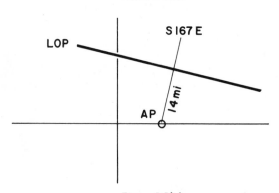

Figure 8-3(b).

Consider a case where the observed altitude of the sun is $45°38'$, and the tables show Hc = $45°52'$, Z = N167W. Figure 8-3(a) shows Z drawn in the same fashion as the previous examples. In this case, though, *a* is 14 miles away, so we must extend the Z line in the opposite direction in order to lay off and plot the LOP. Far easier, though, is to simply reverse both the prefix and suffix of Z, and then plot in the usual way. Thus N167W becomes S167E. Figure 8-3(b) shows the plot. Note that the reversal of Z is a convenience for plotting only. We have obviously not changed the actual bearing of the sun. This sight would be in the early afternoon, with the sun just west of south.

When plotting an LOP, remember two key points. Z, or its reverse, is laid off from the AP. When setting the dividers to the value of *a*,

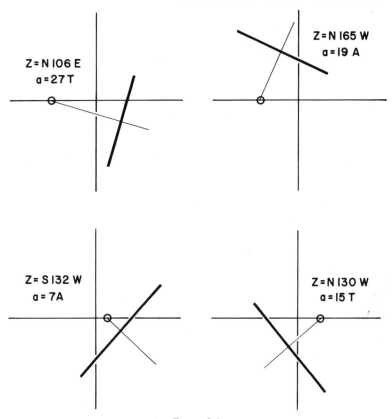

Figure 8-4.

always use the vertical latitude scale. The above examples illustrate a few of the possible combinations.

That's all there is to plotting the LOP itself. Now look at an example that ties all the material in the previous chapters together. A navigator at DR position 28°44′N, 70°06′W takes a morning sight of the sun's lower limb on May 17, 1973. He starts his stopwatch at 14h 28m 00s GMT, and stops it at the instant of the final adjustment of the sextant. The elapsed time is 05m 57s. The sextant reading is 60°22′. The index error is 05′, on the arc. The height of eye is 11 feet. The complete working of this sight is shown below, with the resulting plot of the LOP given in Figure 8-5. The DR position is found to be about 6 miles from the actual LOP. This is not surprising, considering that the DR position may be in error for many reasons, foremost of which is the effect of unknown currents.

	17d	14h	28m	00s
		+	05m	57s
	17d	14h	33m	57s

Sun LL

hs	60°21'
IC	-05'
Dip	-03'
App alt	60°13'
Ref-SD	+15'
Ho	60°28'

	GHA	Dec
17d 14h	33°55'	19°23'N
33m 57s	+8°29'	+0'
	39°24'	19°23'N
aλ	70°24'W	Tab Dec 19° Same
MA	31°E	Tab Hc 60°05'
aL	29°N	cor +10'
		Hc 60°15'

d +25'   Z = N103°E

a = 13T

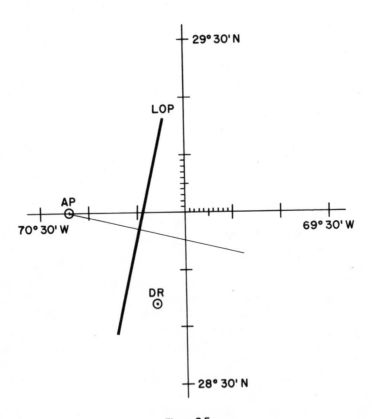

Figure 8-5.

Well, there you have it. In these chapters you've learned how to measure the sun's altitude and calculate your LOP. All of celestial navigation is based upon these few principles. Like many another science, celestial navigation builds upon this foundation a whole structure of details, alternative methods, modifications, solutions for special situations, and refinements for extra accuracy. Some of the most easily applied and useful of these refinements are presented in the rest of this book. None of them, though, displace the basic concepts which you have learned, and which will suffice to lead you, as they have led generations of mariners, to any spot on the globe. The timeless motion of the sun across the sky, and your understanding of its motion, combine to convert the horizon from a barrier to a threshold. Surely no knowledge ever offered greater rewards than that.

9 Lines of Position at Sea

> *At noon, both Carlos and I shot the sun, using the authentic astrolabe and the modern sextant, roughly obtaining our latitude. After several tries, I was able with my fifteenth-century instrument to average within one degree of Carlos' modern sextant.*
>
> Robert Marx, *Voyage of the Nina II*

The navigator's work at sea consists largely in plotting two or more LOP's, and obtaining the vessel's position, or fix, from their intersection. In order to obtain LOP's which result in an accurate fix, a small amount of planning is in order.

The most accurate fix will be obtained when two LOP's intersect at right angles. In this case, an error of 1 mile in one LOP will also put the fix 1 mile from its true position. On the other hand, if the LOP's intersect at a small angle, the same 1-mile error in one LOP will put the fix several miles from its actual location. Figure 9-1 illustrates these two cases.

It is evident that in order to get two LOP's intersecting at a large angle (known as a good "cut"), the sun's bearing must be considerably different for the two sights. An easy way to achieve this is to take one sight in mid-morning, when the sun is in the southeast (for an observer in north latitude), and a second sight in mid-afternoon, when the sun is

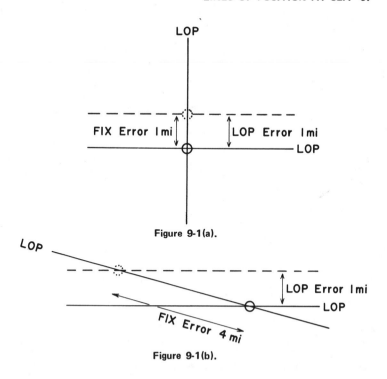

Figure 9-1(a).

Figure 9-1(b).

in the southwest. (If two stars are used, intersecting LOP's can be obtained at one time by using stars in different parts of the sky. Star sights are covered in Chapter 10.) Figure 9-2 shows the resulting Z's and LOP's. Note that it's not necessary to have the LOP's at exactly right angles, although this can be arranged by using the tables to plan the time between the two sights.

If a navigator on a vessel at anchor took morning and afternoon sights and plotted the LOP's, as shown in Figure 9-2, things would work out nicely and give a good fix. The catch here, of course, is that fixes are rarely needed while at anchor. On the other hand, if the vessel is underway, the LOP plotted from the morning sight is no longer directly applicable to the afternoon sight, because the vessel has moved during the several hours between sights and is no longer on the morning LOP. This situation is dealt with easily enough, though, by *advancing the LOP* of the morning sight. This simply means that you shift the morning LOP the same distance and in the same direction as the vessel has moved since the morning sight.

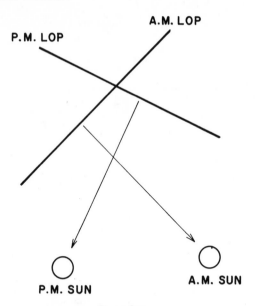

Figure 9-2.

For example, assume that the morning sight is taken at 09:00 ship's time, and the afternoon sight is taken at 15:00 ship's time. During the day the ship has been sailing west (remember to make the variation correction if you're steering by magnetic compass) at an average speed of 7 knots. Since 6 hours have elapsed between sights, the ship has moved west 42 miles. Shift the morning LOP westward, also by 42 miles. This is the 09:00 advanced LOP, and is so labeled. Its intersection with the 15:00 LOP gives the 15:00 position, called a running fix. Figure 9-3 illustrates this case.

What if you change course and/or speed between the two sights? No great problem. Make a plot of the DR track between the times of the first and second sights. A line between the first and last DR positions gives the course and distance made good, to be used in advancing the earlier LOP. The effect of estimated current may also be allowed for.

To illustrate this, assume that a morning sight is taken at 09:30 ship's time. The course is 155° and the speed is 6 knots. At 11:00, the course is changed to 064° and the speed becomes 7 knots. At 16:00, another sight is taken for the afternoon LOP. It is estimated that the current has been setting all day in a direction of 317° (set) at a speed of 2.3 knots (drift). How much must the morning LOP be advanced, and in what direction? The 09:30 LOP is plotted. The 09:30 DR

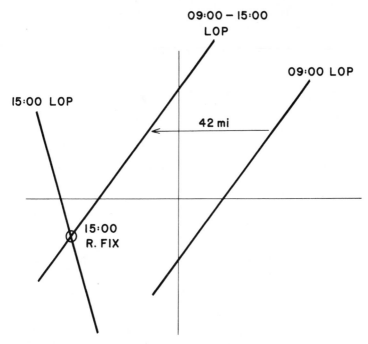

09:00 − 15:00
LOP

09:00 LOP

15:00 LOP

42 mi

15:00
R. FIX

Figure 9-3.   A running fix.

position is also plotted, probably being carried forward from a fix of the previous evening. From 09:30 to 11:00 the ship will move 9 miles (1 1/2 hours at 6 knots) on a course of 155°. This locates the 11:00 DR position. From 11:00 to 16:00, the ship will move 35 miles (5 hours at 7 knots) on a course of 064°, which locates the 16:00 DR position. Note that the current has not been considered so far. However, it is now estimated that the current has been setting in a 317° direction at a rate of 2.3 knots. This has been affecting the ship the entire time, so due to current alone the ship will have moved 15 miles (6 1/2 hours at 2.3 knots) in a direction of 317°. This movement, applied to the 16:00 DR position, results in an estimated position (EP) for 16:00. Note that the DR positions may be quite accurate, if the course has been carefully steered and the ship's speed accurately known. The estimate of the current, which may derive from current tables, pilot chart, or pure hunch, is still only an estimate. Nevertheless, it is applied to the DR position, resulting in an EP which is almost certainly more accurate than if the current had been ignored. Finally, draw a line between the 09:30 DR position and the 16:00 EP. This is the course made good

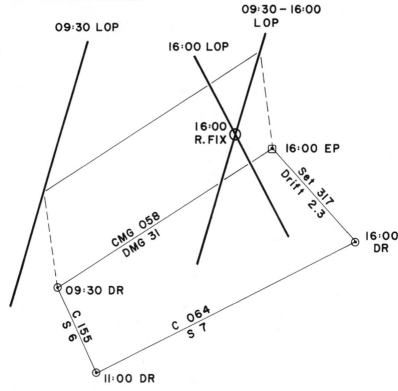

Figure 9-4.

(CMG) and measures 058°. The length of the line is the distance made good (DMG) and measures 31 miles. Therefore the 09:30 LOP must be advanced 31 miles in a direction of 058°. The intersection of the advanced 09:30 LOP with the 16:00 LOP gives the 16:00 running fix. Figure 9-4 shows the plot of the above figures. Note that in the plot each line and position drawn is labeled, except for the line parallel to the CMG, which is shown here for illustration only and is normally not drawn.

NOON LATITUDE SIGHTS

As mentioned in Chapter 2, the noon latitude sight has always been popular due to its simplicity. Let's see just how this type of sight is worked out.

First of all, you will need to work out in advance the approximate time that the sun will make its meridian passage, reaching its highest point in the sky due south of you. The almanac gives the time of this event in local time. You will have to adjust this unless you happen to be located on a standard meridian, i.e., an exact multiple of 15°. For example, if the time of meridian passage is listed as 12:06, and your longitude is about 50°W, the meridian passage will occur later than 12:06 since you are west of the nearest standard meridian, 45°W. The sun's GP moves 15 degrees per hour, or 1 degree every 4 minutes of time, and you are 5 degrees west of the standard meridian, so you must add 20 minutes to the listed time. At your location, then, the sun's meridian passage should occur about 12:26.

About 15 minutes before this time you measure the sun's altitude in the usual way. After a couple of minutes, measure it again and you will find it has increased. As you keep measuring, it will continue increasing, but more and more slowly. Finally it will stop increasing, hang nearly fixed for a minute or two, and then begin decreasing. The maximum reading marks the meridian passage. Record the reading and the time. You will probably find that the time corresponds quite nicely to your advance calculation. Now correct the sextant reading (hs) to the observed altitude (Ho) in the usual way. Convert the local time of meridian passage to GMT (or record the time in GMT) and look up the Dec of the sun for this time. Remember to watch the Greenwich date.

To determine the latitude, subtract Ho from 90°. The resulting quantity is called z. Combining z with the sun's declination gives your latitude. It's as simple as that. For example suppose that Ho is 52°15', and the sun's declination is 12°26'N. The work will look like this:

$$
\begin{array}{ll}
89°60' & \\
- \underline{52°15'} & Ho \\
37°45' & z \\
+ \underline{12°26'} & N\ Dec \\
50°11' & N\ Lat \\
\end{array}
$$

Why is the declination added to z? It isn't always added. Just remember that z is essentially a measure of how far around the earth you are located from the sun's GP. However, you want to know how far you are from the equator. If you are 30° north of the sun, and the sun is 10° north of the equator, it follows that you are 40° north of the equator. Conversely, if you are 50° north of the sun, but the sun is 15° south of the equator, you are only 35° north of the equator. In practice you will have at least an approximate idea of your latitude, so it will be obvious whether to add or subtract the declination.

Notice that the time is used only to determine the sun's declination, which never changes faster than 1 minute of arc per hour. This is the reason that the time needn't be known exactly, which made the method popular with early navigators who didn't have the accurate time at their disposal as readily as we have today.

There's another reason for the noon sight's popularity. As you know, two LOP's are required to determine a fix. The noon sight gives an LOP with a good deal less work than usual. This can be combined with an LOP advanced from early morning to give the noon position. The saving in work is substantial, and was even more considerable for early ship captains who didn't have the advantage of sight reduction tables to simplify their calculations. For this reason, the noon sight was standard practice, and the ship's run was reported from noon to noon.

LANDFALLS

> *Fortunately the sun had risen nearly dead ahead; a sun observation would give me a position line which would decide how far up the coast I was. I hurredly fished out the sextant and set to work.*

> Francis Chichester, *Gipsy Moth Circles the World*

It's quite true that you need two LOP's to determine a fix, but that doesn't mean that a single LOP isn't useful. Suppose you're approaching a coast from seaward, and you'd like to know how far off you are. If the coast runs in a northwest direction, a sight taken in the afternoon when the sun is in the southwest will give an LOP which runs parallel to the coast. This single LOP does not fix your position, but it does show immediately your distance of (see Figure 9-5[a]).

What if the only available LOP doesn't parallel the coast, but intersects it at an angle? Such a case is shown in Figure 9-5(b). Obviously the distance off can't be found from this LOP, but a couple of other useful things can be. First, of all the courses that you might consider steering, a course of $020°$, which is along the LOP, would be a poor choice indeed, since it would lead you onto the reef near shore. Second, if your destination is the harbor, you can determine a way to reach it. Advance the LOP so that it intersects the harbor. If you now arrange to place your vessel on the advanced LOP, you can sail along it on a course of $020°$ to reach the harbor. You have several options to get from your present LOP to the advanced LOP. You might sail 20 miles on a course of 250°. This is guaranteed safe, since you parallel the coast, but is not the shortest route. If you have some knowledge of your distance off, you might elect to sail 15 miles on a course of 295°, which requires 19 miles less sailing to reach harbor. Another useful application of a single LOP is checking your compass. When you take a sun sight and work out Hc and Z, you normally use Z to plot the LOP. Don't overlook the fact that Z is also a very accurate measure of the sun's bearing from the AP. Since you will be located somewhere near the AP, the sun's bearing will be essentially the same at your position, and this known bearing can be used to check the compass.

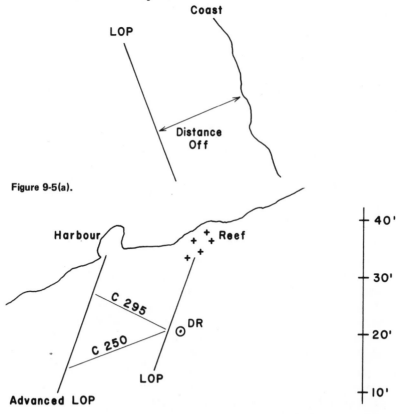

Figure 9-5(a).

Figure 9-5(b).

To use the azimuth angle (Z) for this purpose, you must first convert it to azimuth (Zn). The best way to do this is with a small sketch and

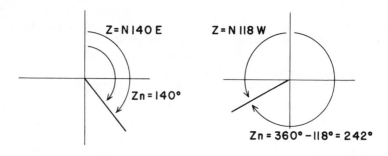

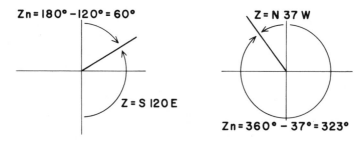

Figure 9-6.

some common sense, remembering that Zn is measured from north clockwise through 360 degrees, just like a compass rose. Some examples are shown in Figure 9-6.

Once you have found the sun's bearing, Zn, what to do with it? Well, compare it with the bearing indicated on your compass, of course. But you have to remember that even a perfect compass won't usually show the same figure, and the reason is *variation*. Variation is the difference, given in degrees, between geographic (true) north and magnetic north. It's caused by the large distance, about 900 miles, between the earth's North Pole and the Magnetic North Pole. The variation figure for a particular location can be found on a chart of the area. It must be added or subtracted, depending on whether the variation is west or east. If the chart gives both magnetic and true compass roses, these provide a simple way of making the conversion. If not, remember the rule:

Variation East, Compass Least (i.e. Magnetic less than True)
Variation West, Compass Best (Magnetic more than True)

Having converted the magnetic compass bearing to a true bearing, compare this with the calculated value of *Zn.* If they're the same, your compass is correct as to that heading. If not, the difference represents *compass deviation,* usually caused by iron or steel near the compass. The amount of deviation should be recorded for future reference. If accurate compass courses must be steered, check the deviation on at least four different headings, and preferably eight.

DISTANCE OFF BY VERTICAL ANGLE

Offshore navigation is generally a pretty leisurely business. Hazards are few and far between, and there's plenty of time to take sights, work them out, and check any discrepancies. A fix once a day is enough. On the other hand, when you're doing coastwise piloting, you often need to fix your position in a hurry. Of course, if you have two known objects in view, you can take cross-bearings and plot them, as shown in almost every book written on navigation and piloting. This works fine as long as you know where you are; there will be a regular forest of lighthouses, beacons, and radio masts to take bearings on. There's a catch, of course: as soon as you feel a bit lost and want to fix your position, those objects will conspire to vanish or become unidentifiable.

As long as you have one object in view, you can get a position line by using your sextant to measure the vertical angle. This takes no trouble at all and requires no tables. Combined with a compass bearing on the object, it gives you an accurate fix quickly and easily.

Charts pinpoint the location of lighthouses accurately; they also list information about the light, such as color, interval, and height above the water. This last is the key to using vertical angle measurements. With your sextant, measure the altitude of the lantern by "bringing it down" to the water's edge, just like taking a sun sight. Read the sextant angle (hs) and correct for index error. If the angle is more than 60', convert the degrees and minutes into minutes. For example, $2°17'$ would convert to 137'. With the known height of the light in feet, and the sextant angle in minutes, the formula

$$D = \frac{.565 \times H}{M}$$

is used to find the distance off in nautical miles. For example, if the light has a height of 85 feet, and the corrected sextant angle is 16', the distance off is found as

$$D = \frac{.565 \times 85}{16}$$

which works out to 3 nautical miles. Nothing could be much simpler than that! Remember that the altitude of the light is measured from the water, not from the base of the light. If the light is beyond your visible horizon, the simple formula above no longer applies. The measured angle will be too small, and the distance off too large.

One other detail could be significant in some situations. The charted height of the light is measured above mean high water. When the tide is at some lower stage, the measured altitude will be greater, resulting in a distance figure that is less than the actual distance. In most circumstances this provides a safety factor, since you will be farther from shore than your calculation indicates. However, if you're passing on the *inside* of some hazard, such as a reef, the extra distance from the light puts you closer to the reef. It's well to remember this.

Now that you have a distance figure, you can plot it on the chart as a circle of position, centered at the light. The radius of the circle will be the calculated distance. To find your position on the circle, take a compass bearing, convert it to true, and plot it. The intersection of the bearing with the circle gives your position.

For example, assume that you are on a course of 034° magnetic, and at 21:10 you sight a light whose charted height is 110 feet. The sextant angle (hs) is 16′, and the index error is 04′ on the arc. The bearing to the light is 294° magnetic, and in your vicinity the variation is 18° west. You want to plot your position and check for dangers.

The vertical angle in this case is 12′. The distance off is calculated as

$$D = \frac{.565 \times 110}{12}$$

which works out to 5.2 nautical miles. A circle of this radius is drawn on the chart. Now convert the magnetic readings to true. The rule in this case is "variation west, compass best." Accordingly, your course is 016° true, and the bearing to the light is 276° true. The bearing from the light to you will be the reciprocal; 276° – 180°, or 096°. Draw a line from the light in a direction of 096°. Its intersection with the distance circle is your position at 21:20, and is so marked. Now plot your true course from the 21:20 fix. It is obvious that if you maintain this course, you will pass very close to Keelcrunch Reef, so the prudent move is to alter course. Figure 9-7 shows the plot of this work.

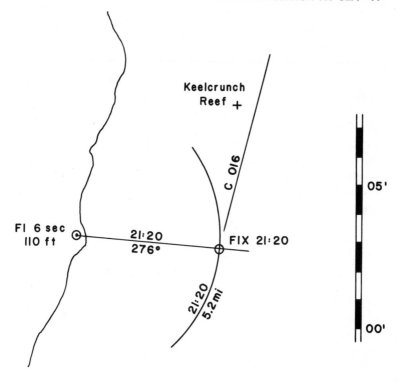

Figure 9-7.

GREAT CIRCLE ROUTES

The shortest distance between two points is not a straight line; not when the two points are on the curved surface of the earth. In such a case, the shortest route is a great circle route. This is the path you would trace out if you cut a globe in half, with the cut going through the two points and the center. Now, carrying a supply of globes to cut up isn't the most practical sort of approach, but there are several other systems.

First of all, consider whether you even need to bother about a great circle route. The equator, and all meridians, are great circles by definition. So if you're sailing in a generally north-south direction at any latitude, or in any direction near the equator, you're automatically on a great circle route, or close enough to make no difference. Only on a generally east-west course at higher latitudes does the question become significant. For example, at latitude 40°, a great circle route between two points 350 miles apart is shorter than a straight line by about 1 mile.

If conditions indicate that you should consider a great circle route, you can quickly get an approximate idea of the route by looking at a standard ocean pilot chart, available from any chart dealer. They show the regular steamer routes between many ports, and these are great circle routes.

Another easy way to work out a great circle route is to use a special chart projection known as gnomonic (no mon' ic). A gnomonic chart looks like no chart you've ever seen, or hope to see.   Latitude lines are curved, land shapes are distorted, and you can't measure distance or direction in the usual way.   But it has one (and only one) redeeming feature: when you draw a straight line between two places, you have the great circle route. Then you can transfer the line, bit by bit, onto a regular Mercator chart. It will appear curved toward the nearer pole. This process is easy, but getting gnomonic charts is hard. Most chart dealers have never heard of them.

The remaining method of working out a great circle route is by means of calculation. This method can appear extremely complicated, and usually does. It can also be very simple. In point of fact, you already know the method. It's only a matter of realizing that you know. Take the point of departure as an AP, and the destination as a GP. Then use the tables in the normal way to find Hc and Z. The great circle course is Z, and by convention we convert it to Zn − i.e., N90°W equals 270°. Hc needn't be used at all, but if you're curious about the distance to the destination, subtract Hc from 90° and convert the remainder to minutes. This is the distance in nautical miles.

How can something so easy be made to look hard? Stretch a string between London and Halifax on a globe to show the great circle route. You will see that the angle between the string and the meridians is different at each meridian. The change is continuous, so if you wanted to follow a great circle route exactly, you would have to continuously change course. That isn't practical, and the normal solution is to follow a series of straight lines that stay close to the great circle route, changing course at regular intervals. Once every 5° or 10° of longitude would be typical. Now, it is possible to mathematically calculate the whole thing out in advance, and that is where the trouble starts. You get into a maze of calculations that would scare anybody off. If you don't believe it, look at the examples in the introduction of HO 211. And it's likely to be wasted effort. If your calculation says that the first change of course should occur at point B, and you find that you've passed point B, you're not about to reverse course to get back to it.

It is also possible to *not* calculate the whole thing in advance, and that is where the trouble ends. Working on this basis, you simply sail for a convenient length of time. Then use your present position, which you know from keeping your navigation up to date, as a departure point and work out a new great circle course.

Now an example. Suppose we're going to sail from Dakar (14°41'N, 17°26'W) to Barbados (13°10'N, 59°26'W). Round off the positions to whole degrees — 15°N, 17°W and 13°N, 59°W. The difference of longitudes — 42°W — is used as a meridian angle. Enter the tables with a latitude of 15°, a Declination of 13° Same Name, and a meridian angle of 42°W. See the extract below.

DECLINATION (0°-14°) <u>SAME</u> NAME AS LATITUDE   LAT 15°

	11°			12°			13°			14°		
LHA	Hc	d	Z	Hc	d	Z	Hc	d	Z	Hc	d	Z
	° ′	′	°	° ′	′	°	° ′	′	°	° ′	′	°
0	86 00	+60	180	87 00	+60	180	88 00	+60	180	89 00	+60	180
1	85 53	58	166	86 51	56	162	87 47	50	154	88 37	25	136
2	85 33	53	154	86 26	47	147	87 13	36	136	87 49	15	117
3	85 03	46	144	85 49	39	135	86 28	28	124	86 56	10	109
4	84 25	40	135	85 05	33	127	85 38	22	117	86 00	8	104
35	55 42	+10	92	55 52	+9	91	56 01	+7	89	56 08	+6	87
36	54 44	10	92	54 54	9	90	55 03	7	89	55 10	6	87
37	53 46	10	92	53 56	9	90	54 05	7	88	54 12	6	87
38	52 48	10	92	52 58	9	90	53 07	8	88	53 15	6	87
39	51 50	10	91	52 00	9	90	52 09	8	88	52 17	6	86
40	50 52	+10	91	51 02	+9	89	51 11	+8	88	51 19	+6	86
41	49 54	10	91	50 04	9	89	50 13	8	88	50 21	6	86
42	48 56	11	90	49 07	8	89	49 15	8	87	49 23	7	86
43	47 58	11	90	48 09	9	89	48 18	7	87	48 25	7	86
44	47 01	10	90	47 11	9	88	47 20	8	87	47 28	6	86
45	46 03	+10	90	46 13	+9	88	46 22	+8	87	46 30	+7	85
46	45 05	10	89	45 15	9	88	45 24	8	87	45 32	7	85
47	44 07	10	89	44 17	9	88	44 26	8	86	44 34	8	85
48	43 09	10	89	43 19	9	88	43 28	9	86	43 37	7	85
49	42 11	10	89	42 21	9	87	42 30	9	86	42 39	7	85

For Hc and Z we obtain 49°15' and N87°W. We convert N87°W to obtain an initial course of 273° True, but when we lay this off on the chart we find that it goes smack over the island of San Tiago. Accordingly, we change the course to 277° True to clear the island. From the North Atlantic Pilot Chart, we find that magnetic variation in this area is 15°W, which gives us our initial compass course (variation west, compass best) of 292° Magnetic. For the distance to be sailed, we subtract Hc from 90°, obtaining 40°45', which equals 2445' or 2445 nautical miles.

Off we go, keeping a careful eye on the navigation to be sure of clearing the island. After several days of sailing, we find that we have passed the island, and are located at 16°N, 25°W. Time for a new course. The meridian angle has now decreased to 34°W. Entering the tables with latitude 16°, Declination 34° Same Name, and meridian angle 34°W, we find Hc = 56°59' and Z = N91°W. Thus our course is 269° True. Notice that we are now headed slightly south of west; thus we have passed the most northern part of the great circle route − the "vertex". Variation in the vicinity is 16°W, giving a compass course of 285° Magnetic.

After a few weeks of sailing with more such course changes, we find that Barbados is only 150 miles ahead. We then abandon great circle calculations, and lay off a course directly to the island.

The example above was picked so that the latitude of the destination was within the Declination range of HO 249 tables. More often, you want to work out a great circle route for high latitudes. In such cases, HO 249 is not suitable. Other tables can be used, such as HO 214 or its successor HO 229. More satisfactory, though, is HO 211. All three of these types of tables are covered in chapter 11. The examples there are in terms of sight reductions, but the tables work just the same for great circle routes.

PLOTTING SHEETS

There are two types of plotting sheets useful to the sailor. One is suitable only for a particular latitude, and is useful for practice sights which are done at one location, as well as short cruises in home waters. The other type is slightly less convenient to use, but is applicable at any latitude. The method of construction of both types is given here.

To understand the basic principle behind a plotting sheet (or any chart or map, for that matter), visualize the earth as a peeled orange. The divisions between segments represent lines of longitude. They are equally spaced around the equator, and converge at the poles. The distance between lines of *longitude,* then, varies from maximum at the equator to zero at the poles. Lines of *latitude,* however, are not subject to this variable spacing. Running horizontally around the earth, they are equally spaced from the equator to the poles. The result is that the relative distance between longitude lines and latitude lines depends on the latitude. When making a plotting sheet, this must be accounted for.

FIXED LATITUDE PLOTTING SHEET

To illustrate the method of construction, a plotting sheet for latitude 53°N is shown in Figure 9-8. Turn a sheet of typing paper on its side. Draw a horizontal line across the middle, for latitude 53°. Draw another line vertically up the center. This line must be divided into equal spaces representing minutes of latitude. A convenient scale for practice sheets is 8 or 10 minutes per inch, with every fifth minute accented. To lay off the longitude scale, use a compass to draw a light line from the 30′ latitude mark downward. With a protractor, carefully mark the 53° point on this arc. Drop a vertical line from the mark to the 53° latitude line. This is the 30′ point on the longitude scale. Now erase the compass arc, and divide the longitude scale into 30 equal parts, accenting fifth and tenth minutes. Extend the scale another 30 minutes if space permits. If you are doing most of your practice sights in one place, it's very convenient to mark the position of your practice location on the sheet. This can be accurately determined from a large scale chart or topographic map of the area. Make a few dozen photocopies. When you take a practice sight and plot the LOP, you can immediately check the accuracy of the work.

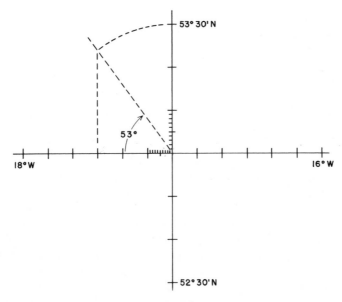

Figure 9-8.

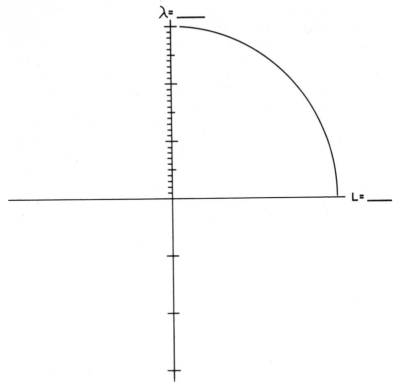

Figure 9-9.

UNIVERSAL PLOTTING SHEET

These sheets can be used at any latitude, and thus are useful on longer cruises. Construction of the sheets is very simple. The vertical latitude scale is marked off as before, but is not labeled. The compass arc is drawn permanently, and the horizontal longitude line carries no markings. Figure 9-9 shows the layout. Draw your own version and make some photocopies.

To use one of these sheets, first choose the central latitude nearest to your position and mark it on the sheet. Draw a radius out to the compass arc, at an angle equal to the central latitude. Where the radius meets the arc, drop a vertical line to the central latitude line to define the 30′ point. Label the point. *Do not make the mistake of using the end of the compass arc as the 30′ point.* It would be possible to divide off the longitude scale, in much the same fashion as the Fixed Latitude

Plotting Sheet. This isn't alwasy easy to do when bouncing around at sea, though, and is not necessary. You can use dividers to measure longitude from the latitude scale, simply by remembering that a given number of minutes of latitude has a certain length on the latitude scale. This length along the radius to the compass arc, projected down to the longitude scale, represents the same number of minutes of longitude. Figure 9-10 shows this relationship for measuring a longitude of 21′.

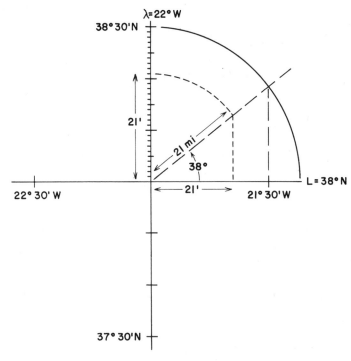

Figure 9-10.

For a check on your technique in plotting LOP's, construct a plotting sheet for latitude 48°N. On this sheet, plot the following three LOP's.

1. AP: 48°N, 32°28′W	Z = S73W	a = 8A
2. AP: 48°N, 31°42′W	Z = N55W	a = 27T
3. AP: 48°N, 32°07′W	Z = N21E	a = 7T

If the work is correctly done, the three LOP's will meet at a point, giving a fix at 48°11′N, 32°21′W. Details of this plot are given in the Appendix.

10 Moon, Planet, and Star Sights

Sunday, June 26th, when, having a fine, clear day, the captain got a lunar observation, as well as his meridian altitude, which made us in lat. 47° 50' S., lon. 113° 49' W.

R. H. Dana, *Two Years Before the Mast*

MOON SIGHTS

The moon has always been popular with lovers, but not always so with navigators. There's a notion around that the moon isn't useful for sights, because it "moves fast" or some such. It's a pity this mistaken idea still hangs on. After all, the moon is big and bright and everybody recognizes it. Moreover, it's visible in the night sky for about half of every month. That's more than can be said for the planets or stars. A moon sight is basically the same as a sun sight. There are a few differences in details, which are explained in this chapter.

First of all, you may have to make either an upper limb observation or a lower limb observation, depending on the phase of the moon. Just read the sextant angle and note whether the observation is upper limb (UL) or lower limb (LL) (see Figure 10-1). Having made your observation and noted the time, you must find the GP of the moon at that time. The GP is given in the Almanac in terms of GHA and declination, just as for the sun. The daily page figures, though, require a couple of corrections to allow for the fact that the GHA doesn't increase at a constant rate, and the declination changes quite rapidly.

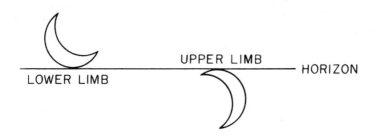

Figure 10-1.

Consider a moon sight taken at May 16, 1973, GMT 11h 56m 07s. Extracts from the Almanac are given below:

1973 MAY 16, 17, 18 (WED., THURS., FRI.) **56ᵐ** INCREMENTS AND CORRECTIONS

G.M.T.	SUN		MOON				
	G.H.A.	Dec.	G.H.A.	v	Dec.	d	H.P.
d h	° ′	° ′	° ′	′	° ′	′	′
16 00	180 55·5	N19 01·0	15 47·6	12·6	S19 24·7	8·1	54·6
01	195 55·5	01·6	30 19·2	12·5	19 32·8	7·9	54·6
02	210 55·5	02·2	44 50·7	12·4	19 40·7	7·9	54·6
03	225 55·5 ··	02·8	59 22·1	12·4	19 48·6	7·8	54·6
04	240 55·5	03·4	73 53·5	12·4	19 56·4	7·7	54·5
05	255 55·5	03·9	88 24·9	12·3	20 04·1	7·7	54·5
06	270 55·5	N19 04·5	102 56·2	12·3	S20 11·8	7·5	54·5
W 07	285 55·5	05·1	117 27·5	12·3	20 19·3	7·4	54·5
E 08	300 55·5	05·7	131 58·8	12·2	20 26·7	7·3	54·5
D 09	315 55·5 ··	06·3	146 30·0	12·2	20 34·0	7·3	54·5
N 10	330 55·4	06·8	161 01·2	12·2	20 41·3	7·1	54·5
E 11	345 55·4 ·	07·4	175 32·4	12·1	20 48·4	7·0	54·5
S 12	0 55·4	N19 08·0	190 03·5	12·0	S20 55·4	7·0	54·4
D 13	15 55·4	08·6	204 34·5	12·1	21 02·4	6·8	54·4
A 14	30 55·4	09·1	219 05·6	12·0	21 09·2	6·7	54·4
Y 15	45 55·4 ··	09·7	233 36·6	12·0	21 15·9	6·7	54·4
16	60 55·4	10·3	248 07·6	11·9	21 22·6	6·5	54·4

56ᵐ	SUN PLANETS	ARIES	MOON	v or Corrⁿ d		v or Corrⁿ d		v or Corrⁿ d	
s	° ′	° ′	° ′	′	′	′	′	′	′
00	14 00·0	14 02·3	13 21·7	0·0	0·0	6·0	5·7	12·0	11·3
01	14 00·3	14 02·6	13 22·0	0·1	0·1	6·1	5·7	12·1	11·4
02	14 00·5	14 02·8	13 22·2	0·2	0·2	6·2	5·8	12·2	11·5
03	14 00·8	14 03·1	13 22·4	0·3	0·3	6·3	5·9	12·3	11·6
04	14 01·0	14 03·3	13 22·7	0·4	0·4	6·4	6·0	12·4	11·7
05	14 01·3	14 03·6	13 22·9	0·5	0·5	6·5	6·1	12·5	11·8
06	14 01·5	14 03·8	13 23·2	0·6	0·6	6·6	6·2	12·6	11·9
07	14 01·8	14 04·1	13 23·4	0·7	0·7	6·7	6·3	12·7	12·0
08	14 02·0	14 04·3	13 23·6	0·8	0·8	6·8	6·4	12·8	12·1
09	14 02·3	14 04·6	13 23·9	0·9	0·8	6·9	6·5	12·9	12·1
10	14 02·5	14 04·8	13 24·1	1·0	0·9	7·0	6·6	13·0	12·2
11	14 02·8	14 05·1	13 24·4	1·1	1·0	7·1	6·7	13·1	12·3
12	14 03·0	14 05·3	13 24·6	1·2	1·1	7·2	6·8	13·2	12·4
13	14 03·3	14 05·6	13 24·8	1·3	1·2	7·3	6·9	13·3	12·5
14	14 03·5	14 05·8	13 25·1	1·4	1·3	7·4	7·0	13·4	12·6

Copy down all the figures given on the 11h line of the daily page. The value of v is always positive, but the value of d (which is just the difference in declination from hour to hour) may be either positive or negative. You must check which by noting whether the declination is increasing or decreasing. In the present case it is increasing, so d is positive. The increase in GHA during the 56m 07s must be allowed for, just as for the sun. On the 56m "Increments and Corrections" page, find 07s and read 13°23′ in the "Moon" column. Finally, the v correction must be applied to the GHA, and the d correction applied to the declination. Find the v value, 12.1, in small print and read the v correction in larger print beside it. In this case it is 11′. The d correction is found in the same way to be 7′. Your work, then, will look like this:

	GHA	Dec	HP.
16d 11h	*175°32′ + 12.1*	*20°48′S + 7.0*	*54.5*
56m 07s	*13°23′*		
	+11′	*+7′*	
	189°06′	*20°55′S*	

You now have the correct values of GHA and declination for this sight. Simple enough, isn't it? So much for the myth of the fast-moving moon!

The sextant reading (hs) must be corrected for the same things that you're used to with sun sights, plus one other factor. This is parallax, and it comes about because the moon is much closer to the earth than is the sun. The parallax correction is combined with the refraction and semidiameter corrections in tables on the inside back pages of the Almanac. To illustrate the use of these tables, we'll assume that you have a lower limb moon sight with hs = 25°27′. Index error is 05′ on the arc, and height of eye is 9 feet. IC (–05′) and dip (–03′) are applied exactly as for the sun, resulting in an apparent altitude of 25°19′. Now refer to the extracts from the Almanac shown.

For an apparent altitude of 25°19′, enter the 25° – 29° column, in the 25° section. Round off the 19′ to the nearest 10 minutes, or 20′. Find this value in the left-hand column to determine the correct line. Now read off the value of the first correction, which is 61′. The second correction is found in the lower section of the tables. The value of H.P. (horizontal parallax), which you noted while looking up the GHA and Dec values given in the daily page, is used to determine which line of the tables to use. In this case H.P. was 54.5. The closest tabulated value is 54.6. On this line, in the "L" (lower limb) column under the 25° – 29° column used earlier, find the second correction value, 01′. Both of these corrections are added to the App Alt, so the work looks like this:

hs	*25°27′*	*L.L.*
IC	*–05′*	
Dip	*–03′*	
App Alt	*25°19′*	
	+61′	
	+01′	
Ho	*26°21′*	

So you see that sextant corrections for the moon are very similar to those for the sun, with an additional two steps. Note that in the case of an upper limb moon sight, 30′ must be subtracted from the apparent altitude as well.

ALTITUDE CORRECTION TABLES 0°–35°—MOON

App. Alt.	0°–4° Corrⁿ	5°–9° Corrⁿ	10°–14° Corrⁿ	15°–19° Corrⁿ	20°–24° Corrⁿ	25°–29° Corrⁿ	30°–34° Corrⁿ	App. Alt.
00	0 33·8	5 58·2	10 62·1	15 62·8	20 62·2	25 60·8	30 58·9	00
10	35·9	58·5	62·2	62·8	62·1	60·8	58·8	10
20	37·8	58·7	62·2	62·8	62·1	(60·7)	58·8	20
30	39·6	58·9	62·3	62·8	62·1	60·7	58·7	30
40	41·2	59·1	62·3	62·8	62·0	60·6	58·6	40
50	42·6	59·3	62·4	62·7	62·0	60·6	58·5	50
00	1 44·0	6 59·5	11 62·4	16 62·7	21 62·0	26 60·5	31 58·5	00
10	45·2	59·7	62·4	62·7	61·9	60·4	58·4	10
20	46·3	59·9	62·5	62·7	61·9	60·4	58·3	20
30	47·3	60·0	62·5	62·7	61·9	60·3	58·2	30
40	48·3	60·2	62·5	62·7	61·8	60·3	58·2	40
50	49·2	60·3	62·6	62·7	61·8	60·2	58·1	50

H.P.	L U	L U	L U	L U	L U	L U	L U	H.P.
54·0	0·3 0·9	0·3 0·9	0·4 1·0	0·5 1·1	0·6 1·2	0·7 1·3	0·9 1·5	54·0
54·3	0·7 1·1	0·7 1·2	0·7 1·2	0·8 1·3	0·9 1·4	1·1 1·5	1·2 1·7	54·3
54·6	1·1 1·4	1·1 1·4	1·1 1·4	1·2 1·5	1·3 1·6	(1·4) 1·7	1·5 1·8	54·6
54·9	1·4 1·6	1·5 1·6	1·5 1·6	1·6 1·7	1·6 1·8	1·8 1·9	1·9 2·0	54·9
55·2	1·8 1·8	1·8 1·8	1·9 1·9	1·9 1·9	2·0 2·0	2·1 2·1	2·2 2·2	55·2
55·5	2·2 2·0	2·2 2·0	2·3 2·1	2·3 2·1	2·4 2·2	2·4 2·3	2·5 2·4	55·5
55·8	2·6 2·2	2·6 2·2	2·6 2·3	2·7 2·3	2·7 2·4	2·8 2·4	2·9 2·5	55·8
56·1	3·0 2·4	3·0 2·5	3·0 2·5	3·0 2·5	3·1 2·6	3·1 2·6	3·2 2·7	56·1

MOON CORRECTION TABLE

The correction is in two parts; the first correction is taken from the upper part of the table with argument apparent altitude, and the second from the lower part, with argument H.P., in the same column as that from which the first correction was taken. Separate corrections are given in the lower part for lower (L) and upper (U) limbs. All corrections are to be **added** to apparent altitude, *but 30′ is to be subtracted from the altitude of the upper limb.*

For corrections for pressure and temperature, see page A_4.

For bubble sextant observations ignore dip, take the mean of upper and lower limb corrections and subtract 15′ from the altitude.

App. Alt. = Apparent altitude = Sextant altitude corrected for index error and dip.

Having obtained the GHA and Dec of the moon at the time of the sight, and the observed altitude (Ho), the rest of the sight is worked out and plotted exactly as for a sun sight.

Here are some practice problems. Answers to be found in the Appendix.

1. Find the GHA and Dec of the moon on May 16, 1973, GMT 14h 56m 13s.
2. An upper limb moon sight is taken on May 16, 1973, GMT 13h 00m 00s. The sextant reading hs = 20°43', index error is 03' on the arc, height of eye is 9 feet. Find Ho for this sight.

PLANET SIGHTS

Planet observations are often very convenient for the navigator. At many times in the year, two planets will be visible at once, so that two LOP's may be obtained at the same time. This gives a fix at once, without the necessity of advancing an earlier LOP. Another advantage is that the planets are bright and easily located in the sky.

There are nine principal planets in our solar system: in order, Mercury, Venus, Earth, Mars, Jupiter, Saturn, Uranus, Neptune, and Pluto. Mercury is so close to the sun that it rises and sets at about the same time as the sun; thus the sky is generally too bright for the planet to be seen. Uranus, Neptune, and Pluto are so faint they cannot be seen with the naked eye. We are then left with four planets which are useful to the navigator. These are Venus, Mars, Jupiter, and Saturn. Their GHA and declination values are tabulated on the left-hand daily pages of the Almanac, in much the same fashion as for the sun. The times of meridian passage are also listed, in local time. These figures are useful for determining which planets will be visible at a given time.

Planet sights at sea are best made at morning or evening twilight, when the horizon is visible. If you're using an artificial horizon on land, sights are better done at night, when the planets appear brightest. Locating a planet in the sky is relatively easy. Since all the planets, including Earth, have their orbits in approximately the same plane, the apparent path of a planet through our sky is similar to the apparent path of the sun. By the time you're ready to try a planet sight, you will be quite familiar with the path of the sun at your location and time of year, and thus will have quite a good idea of where to look for a planet. With few exceptions, the planets are brighter than stars, which is quite a help in picking them out.

To illustrate the use of the Almanac in locating a planet, consider a morning sight on June 20, 1973. The times of meridian passage are listed in the lower right corner of the daily page, extracted here.

1973 JUNE 18, 19, 20 (MON., TUES., WED.)

G.M.T. d h	ARIES G.H.A.	VENUS −3.3 G.H.A.	Dec.	MARS +0.1 G.H.A.	Dec.	JUPITER −2.2 G.H.A.	Dec.	SATURN +0.2 G.H.A.	Dec.	STARS Name	S.H.A.	Dec.
20 00	268 03.8	159 04.4	N23 36.0	267 32.1	S 2 39.3	313 55.8	S17 55.7	183 46.3	N22 14.9	Mirfak	309 23.8	N 49 46.0
01	283 06.3	174 03.6	35.7	282 33.1	38.7	328 58.4	55.8	198 48.4	14.9	Nunki	76 35.0	S 26 19.8
02	298 08.7	189 02.7	35.3	297 34.0	38.0	344 01.0	55.8	213 50.5	14.9	Peacock	54 05.7	S 56 49.1
03	313 11.2	204 01.9	.. 35.0	312 34.9	.. 37.4	359 03.6	.. 55.9	228 52.6	.. 14.9	Pollux	244 04.6	N 28 05.5
04	328 13.7	219 01.0	34.7	327 35.9	36.8	14 06.2	55.9	243 54.7	14.9	Procyon	245 31.3	N 5 17.6
05	343 16.1	234 00.2	34.3	342 36.8	36.2	29 08.8	56.0	258 56.8	14.9			
06	358 18.6	248 59.4	N23 34.0	357 37.7	S 2 35.6	44 11.5	S17 56.0	273 59.0	N22 15.0	Rasalhague	96 33.9	N 12 34.7
W 07	13 21.0	263 58.5	33.6	12 38.7	35.0	59 14.1	56.1	289 01.1	15.0	Regulus	208 15.5	N 12 05.8
E 08	28 23.5	278 57.7	33.3	27 39.6	34.4	74 16.7	56.1	304 03.2	15.0	Rigel	281 41.2	S 8 13.8
D 09	43 26.0	293 56.8	.. 33.0	42 40.5	.. 33.8	89 19.3	.. 56.2	319 05.3	.. 15.0	Rigil Kent.	140 32.3	S 60 43.9
N 10	58 28.4	308 56.0	32.6	57 41.5	33.2	104 21.9	56.3	334 07.4	15.0	Sabik	102 46.6	S 15 41.7
E 11	73 30.9	323 55.1	32.3	72 42.4	32.5	119 24.6	56.3	349 09.5	15.0			
S 12	88 33.4	338 54.3	N23 31.9	87 43.4	S 2 31.9	134 27.2	S17 56.4	4 11.6	N22 15.0	Schedar	350 15.0	N 56 23.4
D 13	103 35.8	353 53.5	31.6	102 44.3	31.3	149 29.8	56.4	19 13.7	15.1	Shaula	97 02.2	S 37 05.2
A 14	118 38.3	8 52.6	31.2	117 45.2	30.7	164 32.4	56.5	34 15.9	15.1	Sirius	259 00.5	S 16 40.8
Y 15	133 40.8	23 51.8	.. 30.9	132 46.2	.. 30.1	179 35.1	.. 56.5	49 18.0	.. 15.1	Spica	159 02.7	S 11 01.6
16	148 43.2	38 51.0	30.5	147 47.1	29.5	194 37.7	56.6	64 20.1	15.1	Suhail	223 14.9	S 43 19.7
17	163 45.7	53 50.1	30.2	162 48.0	28.9	209 40.3	56.6	79 22.2	15.1			
18	178 48.2	68 49.2	N23 29.8	177 49.0	S 2 28.3	224 42.9	S17 56.7	94 24.3	N22 15.1	Vega	80 58.8	N 38 45.4
19	193 50.6	83 48.4	29.5	192 49.9	27.7	239 45.6	56.7	109 26.4	15.2	Zuben'ubi	137 38.4	S 15 56.1
20	208 53.1	98 47.6	29.1	207 50.9	27.1	254 48.2	56.8	124 28.5	15.2		S.H.A.	Mer. Pass.
21	223 55.5	113 46.7	.. 28.8	222 51.8	.. 26.5	269 50.8	.. 56.8	139 30.7	.. 15.2		° ′	h m
22	238 58.0	128 45.9	28.4	237 52.7	25.8	284 53.4	56.9	154 32.8	15.2	Venus	252 20.2	13 23
23	254 00.5	143 45.0	28.1	252 53.7	25.2	299 56.1	56.9	169 34.9	15.2	Mars	0 05.1	6 11
Mer. Pass.	6 10.7	v −0.8	d 0.3	v 0.9	d 0.6	v 2.6	d 0.1	v 2.1	d 0.0	Jupiter	45 48.3	3 08
										Saturn	275 50.9	11 47

Note that the meridian passage of Mars occurs at 06h 11m. This means that at about 6:00 in the morning (local time, remember) Mars will be high in the sky, bearing south. It will be somewhat lower in the sky than the sun is at noon, since at this date the declination of the sun is about 23°N, while Mars is about 2°S. Look for a bright object in this area of the sky; it will almost certainly be Mars. The reddish tinge of Mars is another aid to identification.

Now note that the meridian passage of Jupiter occurs at 03h 08m. Since it is due south at 3:00 in the morning, by 6:00 in the morning it will be in the west and setting. Again, its declination of 17°S is your clue to look for it south of the sun's path. Jupiter is generally quite bright and clear white. With binoculars you may be able to see several of its 12 moons.

The best way to positively identify a planet (or star, for that matter) for the first time is to go ahead and take a sight. If the resulting LOP falls close to your known position, you have the right planet. It affords quite a satisfaction to identify for sure a planet which you may have known only vaguely before; having once done so, you'll find it easy to pick out that planet at a glance.

Question: When you've identified a planet and taken a sight, how to work out the LOP? *Answer:* Even more easily than a moon sight. The GHA and Dec are worked out in just the same fashion as the moon, using *v* and *d* corrections. A small difference here is that *v* and *d* change slowly, so they are listed only once per page, at the bottom of the column. Corrections to the sextant reading are much simpler than for the moon. To illustrate the method, let's put some firm numbers on that June 20 morning sight of Jupiter: GMT 08h 32m 29s, sextant reading 18°42', height of eye 8 feet, index error 04' off the arc.

For the GHA and declination copy down the figures on the 20d 08h line. The *v* and *d* values are found at the bottom of the column. Take the GHA increment and the *v* and *d* corrections from the "Increments and Corrections" tinted section at the back of the Almanac. The value of *v* is positive except occasionally for Venus; these are identified. The *d* value may be either positive or negative; you must check which in the same fashion as for the moon.

32ᵐ   INCREMENTS AND CORRECTIONS   **33ᵐ**

32	SUN PLANETS	ARIES	MOON	v or Corrⁿ / d		v or Corrⁿ / d		v or Corrⁿ / d		33	SUN PLANETS	ARIES	MOON	v or Corrⁿ / d		v or Corrⁿ / d		v or Corrⁿ / d	
s	° '	° '	° '	'	'	'	'	'	'	s	° '	° '	° '	'	'	'	'	'	'
00	8 00·0	8 01·3	7 38·1	0·0	0·0	6·0	3·3	12·0	6·5	00	8 15·0	8 16·4	7 52·5	0·0	0·0	6·0	3·4	12·0	6·7
01	8 00·3	8 01·6	7 38·4	0·1	0·1	6·1	3·3	12·1	6·6	01	8 15·3	8 16·6	7 52·7	0·1	0·1	6·1	3·4	12·1	6·8
02	8 00·5	8 01·8	7 38·6	0·2	0·1	6·2	3·4	12·2	6·6	02	8 15·5	8 16·9	·7 52·9	0·2	0·1	6·2	3·5	12·2	6·8
25	8 06·3	8 07·6	7 44·1	2·5	1·4	8·5	4·6	14·5	7·9	25	8 21·3	8 22·6	7 58·4	2·5	1·4	8·5	4·7	14·5	8·1
26	8 06·5	8 07·8	7 44·3	2·6	1·4	8·6	4·7	14·6	7·9	26	8 21·5	8 22·9	7 58·7	2·6	1·5	8·6	4·8	14·6	8·2
27	8 06·8	8 08·1	7 44·6	2·7	1·5	8·7	4·7	14·7	8·0	27	8 21·8	8 23·1	7 58·9	2·7	1·5	8·7	4·9	14·7	·8·2
28	8 07·0	8 08·3	7 44·8	2·8	1·5	8·8	4·8	14·8	8·0	28	8 22·0	8 23·4	7 59·1	2·8	1·6	8·8	4·9	14·8	8·3
29	8 07·3	8 08·6	7 45·1	2·9	1·6	8·9	4·8	14·9	8·1	29	8 22·3	8 23·6	7 59·4	2·9	1·6	8·9	5·0	14·9	8·3
30	8 07·5	8 08·8	7 45·3	3·0	1·6	9·0	4·9	15·0	8·1	30	8 22·5	8 23·9	7 59·6	3·0	1·7	9·0	5·0	15·0	8·4
31	8 07·8	8 09·1	7 45·5	3·1	1·7	9·1	4·9	15·1	8·2	31	8 22·8	8 24·1	7 59·8	3·1	1·7	9·1	5·1	15·1	8·4

	GHA	v	Dec	d
20d 08h	74°17'	+2.6	17°56'S	+.1
32m 29s	8°07'			
	+01'		+0'	
	82°25ʲ		17°56'S	

To correct the sextant reading, apply IC and dip in the usual way. Planets are so small and so far away that they have no SD or parallax corrections. The only other step is to correct for refraction with the aid of the "Stars and Planets" section on the inside front cover. This appears complete in Table 1, and extracts are given here.

A2 ALTITUDE CORRECTION TABLES 10°-90°—SUN, STARS, PLANETS

OCT.—MAR. **SUN** APR.—SEPT.				STARS AND PLANETS				DIP				
App. Alt.	Lower Limb	Upper Limb	App. Alt.	Lower Limb	Upper Limb	App. Alt.	Corrⁿ	App. Alt.	Additional Corrⁿ	Ht. of Eye	Corrⁿ	Ht. of Eye	Ht. of Eye	Corrⁿ

(table values)

OCT.—MAR. SUN APR.—SEPT.	STARS AND PLANETS	DIP
15 32 +12·9 −19·4 15 59 +13·0 −19·3 16 28 +13·1 −19·2 16 59 +13·2 −19·1 17 32 +13·3 −19·0 18 06 +13·4 −18·9 18 42 +13·5 −18·8	15 46 +12·7 −19·1 16 14 +12·8 −19·0 16 44 +12·9 −18·9 17 15 +13·0 −18·8 17 48 +13·1 −18·7 18 24 +13·2 −18·6 19 01 +13·3 −18·5	16 26 −3·2 16 56 −3·1 17 28 −3·0 18 02 −2·9 18 38 −2·8 19 17 −2·7 19 58 −2·6
		20 +0·6 31 +0·7 **MARS** Jan. 1– June 14	7·5 −4·9 7·9 −5·0 8·2 −5·1 8·5 −5·2 8·8 −5·3 9·2 −5·4 9·5 −5·5	26·0 27·1 28·1 29·2 30·4 31·5	42 −11·4 44 −11·7 46 −11·9 48 −12·2 ft. 2 − 1·4 4 − 1·9

hs	18°42′
IC	+04′
Dip	−03′
App alt	18°43′
Ref	−03′
Ho	18°40′

You now have the values of GHA declination, and Ho. These are used to work out the LOP in exactly the usual way.

Here is a practice problem. Answer to be found in the Appendix.

3. Find the GHA and Dec of Jupiter on June 20, 1973, GMT 18h 33m 02s.

STAR SIGHTS

> *It is astonishing how an ordinary layman comes to know the stars. It is no trouble to steer by them, and much easier to look at them than a compass under a coal oil light.*
>
> Norman Luxton, *Tilikum*

Mention celestial navigation, and the average person will immediately think of stars. The stars are the classic case in celestial navigation, and they have always held a fascination for man. Knowledge of the stars and how to use them is part of the navigator's stock in trade. This section presents some of the methods that are useful.

Before a star can be used for navigation, it must be identified. This is usually the beginner's problem, for the number of stars visible on a clear night beggars description and boggles the mind. Fortunately, there are several systems for bringing order into the apparent chaos. A few pointers, combined with a little thought and a lot of looking, will gradually transform the night sky into a familiar pattern. As you get to know constellations and individual stars at a glance, they take on their own special character and become, as George Mixter so expressively called them, lighthouses in the sky.

The most common method of identifying the stars is with the use of a star chart. These appear in many books in almost as many forms. One is given in the back pages of the Almanac. A similar one, but much larger and with many more stars shown, is published by the National Geographic Society. The price is $2. With any star chart, you must relate what the chart shows to what you see in the sky. Bear in mind that at any particular time of year, you'll be able to see only part of the entire star chart. Even if you watch all night (which you just might, if you catch the fever) only about half of the charted stars will be seen.

The reason for this is that the sun is also in the sky, obviously, and in nearly the same part of the sky each night, not so obviously. The apparent position of the sun moves slowly through the sky, making a complete circuit in a year. The path of this apparent motion of the sun is called the ecliptic, and is shown on most star charts. In the Almanac, the ecliptic is shown on the two "Equatorial Star Charts." For practical purposes, you can label these charts with the months, beginning at the right-hand end with March 21, and advancing one month each division to the left. Thus, you can see that around the end of August, the sun is near the star Regulus. Accordingly, when the earth turns so that you can look in the direction of Regulus, you will also be looking toward the sun, and it's brightness will mask Regulus and the other stars in that part of the sky. This part of the sky, then, can't be seen during the summer, at any time of night, and so is termed the winter sky. Likewise, that section of the sky containing Altair and Markab is termed the summer sky. In the discussion below on relating the visible sky to a star chart, no particular season is assumed. Thus, you must consider the season to know which of the stars mentioned you may expect to see in the sky.

If you're beginning to learn the stars, it's best to begin in a location where the night sky is light enough that not a great many stars are visible. In most cities, a residential section is about right. In this way, only the most prominent stars will be seen, and these will be easily related to a star chart. Once they are familiar, you can move to a darker area where some fainter ones will be seen. But if you begin with a clear night in the country, the great number of stars will overwhelm your star chart and probably you too.

You will notice that the daily pages of the Almanac list 57 stars. These are the so-called "Selected Navigational Stars," which are bright enough and so located as to be useful to the navigator. You might expect to see roughly 10 of these 57 at any particular location and time, and learning 10 stars isn't very difficult. As the seasons progress, it's very interesting to pick out and identify new stars. In the fall, say, you'll probably find yourself staying up until outrageous hours, waiting for a star to rise that wasn't visible during the summer.

For an observer in north latitudes, the best starting place in the sky is the constellation Ursa Major, the familiar Big Dipper. In addition to being very easy to spot, it has the advantage of being a *circumpolar* constellation. That is, at latitudes greater than 45°N, it's visible in the night sky at any time of year. It contains three navigational stars: Alioth and Alkaid in the handle, and Dubhe. Dubhe is the so-called "pointer star," leading the eye in the direction of Polaris, the north star. Polaris has a particular significance in navigation. Since it's located within one degree of the North Celestial Pole, or overhead for an observer at the earth's North Pole, its measured altitude at any point gives the latitude of the point, without calculation, to an accuracy of one degree. For better accuracy, a simple correction table is given in the Almanac; this will be covered later.

The handle of the Dipper forms a smooth curve. If this curve is continued for about the length of the Dipper, it leads very naturally to Arcturus, a bright and useful star. The same curve continued about an equal distance past Arcturus leads to Spica, equally bright and useful. These two stars are best seen in the spring sky.

If you let the eye move from the Big Dipper to Polaris and then an equal distance beyond, you will come to the constellation with a characteristic *W* or *M* shape. This is Cassiopeia. One navigational star, Schedar, is found here. It's not very bright, and so isn't used a great deal, but the constellation is very useful as a pointer to other stars.

Viewed as a *W*, the center star and lower right star (Schedar) form a pointer to Alpheratz, in the constellation Pegasus, the Flying Horse. The four major stars of this constellation form an almost perfect square, which is immediately picked out in the evening fall sky. Markab, about as bright as Alpheratz, is on the opposite corner of the square.

By using the center star of Cassiopeia again, and the lower left star, you have another pointer leading to Mirfak. This star isn't terribly conspicuous at first. Once identified, though, it is seen to be the central part of a very characteristic formation of several stars in a curve. You'll be amazed at how readily the eye can pick out this curve under almost any circumstances.

Near Mirfak you will find Capella, best spotted by its brightness. It's part of the constellation Auriga, which contains four other stars that aren't so bright but can be seen easily enough on a clear night. For some reason, this constellation doesn't stand out as well as others, at least to my eye. Capella is easily found, though, and is helpful in finding some other stars. Find Polaris, then Capella, and then look the same distance again toward the horizon. Here you will find the constellation Orion, the most prominent in the winter sky. Orion, the Great Hunter, is almost as well known as the Big Dipper, and is visible in the winter sky from any point on earth. He is easily seen to have shoulders, a belt and sword, and feet. Not so easily seen are his head and club. His left shoulder (as we see it) is the important navigational star Betelgeuse, which has a noticeably reddish color. His right foot is Rigel, another important star with a bright blue color. His shoulders point left to Procyon. His belt points left to Sirius, the brightest star in the sky. Proceeding from the left end of the belt, past the right shoulder, you come to Aldebaran, somewhat alone in the sky and easily picked out.

Capella has another use as a pointer. Proceed from Capella to Polaris, and then an equal distance beyond. Here you will find Vega, a very bright star with a bluish tinge. Almost the same distance from Polaris as Vega, and fairly near it, you will find Deneb, the tail of the constellation Cygnus, the Swan. Deneb isn't as bright as Vega, but the constellation has an easily seen swan shape. If you don't confuse the head and tail, the swan will be seen to be flying from the eastern to the western horizon.

Vega and Deneb are two stars in an important group of three. Together with Altair, they form the "summer triangle." While this is not a constellation in the proper sense of the word, it is a familiar feature in the summer sky and the three stars are all useful to the navigator. Altair is much lower in the sky, about as far below Vega and Deneb as Polaris is above.

All of the above stars may be found in the various star charts, including the one in the Almanac, and identified in this way. You may also want to use one of the several types of *star finder* that are available. These usually take the form of two discs with a central pivot. One disc has the stars printed on it, and the other is rotated to a position corresponding to a particular time and date. A window then shows which stars are visible in the sky and their positions. One very good star finder is called the Planisphere. It is made in England and distributed by the Planstar Company, 2076 Panorama Drive, North Vancouver, British Columbia. This particular model is made of plastic and is useful because it shows the stars in the same perspective as you see them in the sky. Planispheres are produced in two models covering a range of latitudes suitable for England and also useful in most of North America.

Another star finder, the Model 2102D, has been produced for years by the armed forces and is now available from Weems and Plath, Inc., of Annapolis, Maryland. This model comes with a star base and a set of discs, and so can be used at all latitudes, both north and south. A good feature of the device is that once set, the actual altitudes and azimuths of the stars can be read off with an accuracy of a couple of degrees. It's less convenient than the planisphere to use, though, for two reasons. First, it must be set by consulting the Almanac, because dates and times are not printed on it. Second, only the navigational stars are shown, and they appear reversed from their positions in the sky.

Once you've had enough practice in identifying some of the stars quickly and easily, you'll want to try using them for position sights. The great advantage of using stars is that by choosing three stars in different directions for your sights, you obtain three LOP's that should intersect in a point, defining your position then and there. Usually the LOP's don't intersect exactly, but form a small triangle. The center of this triangle is taken as your position.

Star sights are taken in the same way as planet sights, and the sextant corrections are made in the same way to obtain Ho. The GHA and declination of the stars are listed in the Almanac, but the form of listing is different from the one you're used to. It would be possible to list the GHA and Dec of each star for each hour, in the same fashion as the other bodies, but this would make the Almanac about 50 times bulkier. Fortunately, two simple facts can be used to prevent this.

First of all, the relative positions of all the stars are fixed. Accordingly, the GHA of any star can be found by looking up the GHA of one agreed-upon reference point, and adding the increase in GHA between the reference point and the star of interest. The reference point universally used is the first point of Aries, listed simply as Aries, or by the symbol ♈. This point is not marked by a star, but is the intersection of the ecliptic with the celestial equator. You may find it useful to consider that the sun is located here at the spring equinox, when the declination is 0. At any rate, the GHA of Aries is tabulated in the Almanac for every hour, as with the other bodies. The increment for exact minutes and seconds is given in the tinted "Increments and Corrections" section.

The increase in GHA between Aries and a given star is called the sidereal hour angle (SHA). The SHA for each of the navigational stars is listed in the daily pages. The GHA for a star, then, is found by working out the GHA of Aries, and adding the SHA for the star. This procedure is often summarized by the equation:

$$GHA \text{ ✶} = GHA \text{ ♈} + SHA \text{ ✶}$$

(Note: Some readers may be familiar with the term right ascension (RA), generally used by astronomers. The RA is very similar to SHA, but is measured east from the first point of Aries, and expressed in angular hours of 15°.)

The second simplifying fact derives from the earth's rotation. You're familiar with a rotating gyroscope, which tends to keep its axis pointed always in the same direction. The rotating earth acts like a gyroscope in space, so its axis is always pointed in the same direction in space. Consequently, the declination of the stars is nearly constant, and a star needs its declination listed only once per page for convenient reference. This figure is used without any corrections.

Now let's see how to work out the GHA and declination for the star Altair, on June 18, 1973, GMT 21h 56m 08s. Extracts from the Almanac are given.

1973 JUNE 18, 19, 20 (MON., TUES., WED.)

G.M.T.	ARIES	VENUS −3·3		MARS +0·1		JUPITER −2·2		SATURN +0·2		STARS		
	G.H.A.	G.H.A.	Dec.	G.H.A.	Dec.	G.H.A.	Dec.	G.H.A.	Dec.	Name	S.H.A.	Dec.
d h	° ′	° ′	° ′	° ′	° ′	° ′	° ′	° ′	° ′		° ′	° ′
18 00	266 05·5	159 45·4 N23 50·5		266 47·5 S 3 08·7		311 50·4 S17 53·3		182 04·8 N22 14·1		Acamar	315 41·3	S 40 24·4
01	281 08·0	174 44·5	50·2	281 48·4	08·0	326 53·0	53·4	197 07·0	14·1	Achernar	335 49·1	S 57 21·9
02	296 10·4	189 43·7	49·9	296 49·3	07·4	341 55·6	53·4	212 09·1	14·1	Acrux	173 42·9	S 62 57·6
03	311 12·9	204 42·8 · ·	49·7	311 50·3 · ·	06·8	356 58·3 · ·	53·5	227 11·2 · ·	14·1	Adhara	255 36·4	S 28 56·2
04	326 15·4	219 41·9	49·4	326 51·2	06·2	12 00·9	53·5	242 13·3	14·1	Aldebaran	291 24·1	N 16 27·5
05	341 17·8	234 41·1	49·1	341 52·1	05·6	27 03·5	53·6	257 15·4	14·2			
06	356 20·3	249 40·2 N23 48·8		356 53·0 S 3 05·0		42 06·1 S17 53·6		272 17·5 N22 14·2		Alioth	166 46·6	N 56 06·4
07	11 22·8	264 39·4	48·5	11 54·0	04·4	57 08·7	53·7	287 19·6	14·2	Alkaid	153 22·1	N 49 26·8
08	26 25·2	279 38·5	48·3	26 54·9	03·7	72 11·3	53·7	302 21·7	14·2	Al Na'ir	28 20·9	S 47 05·1
M 09	41 27·7	294 37·7 · ·	48·0	41 55·8 · ·	03·1	87 13·9 · ·	53·8	317 23·9 · ·	14·2	Alnilam	276 17·1	S 1 13·0
O 10	56 30·2	309 36·8	47·7	56 56·8	02·5	102 16·5	53·8	332 26·0	14·2	Alphard	218 25·7	S 8 32·7
N 11	71 32·6	324 35·9	47·4	71 57·7	01·9	117 19·1	53·9	347 28·1	14·3			
D 12	86 35·1	339 35·1 N23 47·1		86 58·6 S 3 01·3		132 21·7 S17 53·9		2 30·2 N22 14·3		Alphecca	126 36·0	N 26 48·2
A 13	101 37·6	354 34·2	46·8	101 59·5	00·7	147 24·3	54·0	17 32·3	14·3	Alpheratz	358 14·6	N 28 56·6
Y 14	116 40·0	9 33·4	46·5	117 00·5	3 00·1	162 26·9	54·0	32 34·4	14·3	Altair	62 37·1	N 8 47·8
15	131 42·5	24 32·5 · ·	46·3	132 01·4	2 59·5	177 29·5 · ·	54·1	47 36·5 · ·	14·3	Ankaa	353 45·2	S 42 26·7
16	146 44·9	39 31·7	46·0	147 02·3	58·8	192 32·1	54·1	62 38·7	14·3	Antares	113 02·7	S 26 22·6
17	161 47·4	54 30·8	45·7	162 03·2	58·2	207 34·7	54·2	77 40·8	14·4			
18	176 49·9	69 29·9 N23 45·4		177 04·2 S 2 57·6		222 37·3 S17 54·2		92 42·9 N22 14·4		Arcturus	146 22·8	N 19 19·2
19	191 52·3	84 29·1	45·1	192 05·1	57·0	237 40·0	54·3	107 45·0	14·4	Atria	108 31·0	S 68 59·0
20	206 54·8	99 28·2	44·8	207 06·0	56·4	252 42·6	54·3	122 47·1	14·4	Avior	234 30·9	S 59 25·7
21	221 57·3	114 27·4 · ·	44·5	222 07·0 · ·	55·8	267 45·2 · ·	54·4	137 49·2 · ·	14·4	Bellatrix	279 04·5	N 6 19·6
22	236 59·7	129 26·5	44·2	237 07·9	55·2	282 47·8	54·4	152 51·3	14·4	Betelgeuse	271 34·1	N 7 24·2
23	252 02·2	144 25·7	43·9	252 08·8	54·6	297 50·4	54·5	167 53·4	14·5			
19 00	267 04·7	159 24·8 N23 43·6		267 09·8 S 2 53·9		312 53·0 S17 54·5		182 55·6 N22 14·5		Canopus	264 10·0	S 52 40·9
01	282 07·1	174 24·0	43·3	282 10·7	53·3	327 55·6	54·6	197 57·7	14·5	Capella	281 19·2	N 45 58·4

56ᵐ INCREMENTS AND CORRECTIONS **57ᵐ**

56ᵐ	SUN PLANETS	ARIES	MOON	v or Corrⁿ d	v or Corrⁿ d	v or Corrⁿ d
s	° ′	° ′	° ′	′ ′	′ ′	′ ′
00	14 00·0	14 02·3	13 21·7	0·0 0·0	6·0 5·7	12·0 11·3
01	14 00·3	14 02·6	13 22·0	0·1 0·1	6·1 5·7	12·1 11·4
02	14 00·5	14 02·8	13 22·2	0·2 0·2	6·2 5·8	12·2 11·5
03	14 00·8	14 03·1	13 22·4	0·3 0·3	6·3 5·9	12·3 11·6
04	14 01·0	14 03·3	13 22·7	0·4 0·4	6·4 6·0	12·4 11·7
05	14 01·3	14 03·6	13 22·9	0·5 0·5	6·5 6·1	12·5 11·8
06	14 01·5	14 03·8	13 23·2	0·6 0·6	6·6 6·2	12·6 11·9
07	14 01·8	14 04·1	13 23·4	0·7 0·7	6·7 6·3	12·7 12·0
08	14 02·0	14 04·3	13 23·6	0·8 0·8	6·8 6·4	12·8 12·1
09	14 02·3	14 04·6	13 23·9	0·9 0·8	6·9 6·5	12·9 12·1

57ᵐ	SUN PLANETS	ARIES	MOON	v or Corrⁿ d	v or Corrⁿ d	v or Corrⁿ d
s	° ′	° ′	° ′	′ ′	′ ′	′ ′
00	14 15·0	14 17·3	13 36·1	0·0 0·0	6·0 5·8	12·0 11·5
01	14 15·3	14 17·6	13 36·3	0·1 0·1	6·1 5·8	12·1 11·6
02	14 15·5	14 17·8	13 36·5	0·2 0·2	6·2 5·9	12·2 11·7
03	14 15·8	14 18·1	13 36·8	0·3 0·3	6·3 6·0	12·3 11·8
04	14 16·0	14 18·3	13 37·0	0·4 0·4	6·4 6·1	12·4 11·9
05	14 16·3	14 18·6	13 37·2	0·5 0·5	6·5 6·2	12·5 12·0
06	14 16·5	14 18·8	13 37·5	0·6 0·6	6·6 6·3	12·6 12·1
07	14 16·8	14 19·1	13 37·7	0·7 0·7	6·7 6·4	12·7 12·2
08	14 17·0	14 19·3	13 38·0	0·8 0·8	6·8 6·5	12·8 12·3
09	14 17·3	14 19·6	13 38·2	0·9 0·9	6·9 6·6	12·9 12·4

18d 21h	GHA ♈ 221°57′
56m 08s	14°04′
Altair	SHA 62°37′ Dec 8°48′N
	298°38′

Altair:	GHA 298°38′
	Dec 8°48′N

The previous example lists more detail than is actually necessary in practical use. The following example is shown in a form which is quite satisfactory to use. For the star Procyon, on December 8, 1973, GMT 01h 33m 47s, the work is as shown.

1973 DECEMBER 6, 7, 8 (THURS., FRI., SAT.)

G.M.T.	ARIES G.H.A.	VENUS −4·3 G.H.A.	Dec.	MARS −1·0 G.H.A.	Dec.	JUPITER −1·7 G.H.A.	Dec.	SATURN +0·2 G.H.A.	Dec.	STARS Name	S.H.A.	Dec.
d h	° ′	° ′	° ′	° ′	° ′	° ′	° ′	° ′	° ′		° ′	° ′
8 00	76 36·5	133 47·5	S22 30·5	52 28·7	N10 37·0	124 25·3	S18 34·5	343 54·7	N22 20·5	Mirfak	309 22·4	N 49 46·4
01	91 39·0	148 48·1	29·9	67 30·9	37·2	139 27·3	34·4	358 57·4	20·5	Nunki	76 35·3	S 26 19·8
02	106 41·5	163 48·6	29·2	82 33·0	37·4	154 29·3	34·3	14 00·1	20·5	Peacock	54 06·1	S 56 49·3
03	121 43·9	178 49·2 ··	28·6	97 35·2 ··	37·7	169 31·3 ··	34·2	29 02·8 ··	20·5	Pollux	244 03·6	N 28 05·3
04	136 46·4	193 49·7	28·0	112 37·3	37·9	184 33·3	34·0	44 05·4	20·6	Procyon	245 30·4	N 5 17·5
05	151 48·8	208 50·3	27·4	127 39·4	38·1	199 35·3	33·9	59 08·1	20·6			
S 06	166 51·3	223 50·8	S22 26·8	142 41·6	N10 38·3	214 37·3	S18 33·8	74 10·8	N22 20·6	Rasalhague	96 34·3	N 12 34·7
A 07	181 53·8	238 51·4	26·1	157 43·7	38·5	229 39·3	33·7	89 13·4	20·6	Regulus	208 14·9	N 12 05·6
T 08	196 56·2	253 51·9	25·5	172 45·8	38·8	244 41·3	33·5	104 16·1	20·6	Rigel	281 40·2	S 8 13·8
U 09	211 58·7	268 52·5 ··	24·9	187 48·0 ··	39·0	259 43·3 ··	33·4	119 18·8 ··	20·6	Rigil Kent.	140 32·8	S 60 43·5
R 10	227 01·2	283 53·1	24·3	202 50·1	39·2	274 45·3	33·3	134 21·5	20·6	Sabik	102 46·9	S 15 41·6
D 11	242 03·6	298 53·6	23·6	217 52·2	39·4	289 47·2	33·2	149 24·1	20·6			
A 12	257 06·1	313 54·2	S22 23·0	232 54·4	N10 39·6	304 49·2	S18 33·0	164 26·8	N22 20·6	Schedar	350 14·2	N 56 24·1
Y 13	272 08·6	328 54·8 *	22·4	247 56·5	39·9	319 51·2	32·9	179 29·5	20·6	Shaula	97 02·6	S 37 05·2
14	287 11·0	343 55·3	21·8	262 58·6	40·1	334 53·2	32·8	194 32·2	20·6	Sirius	258 59·5	S 16 40·7
15	302 13·5	358 55·9 ··	21·1	278 00·7 ··	40·3	349 55·2 ··	32·8	209 34·8 ··	20·6	Spica	159 02·7	S 11 01·6
16	317 16·0	13 56·5	20·5	293 02·9	40·5	4 57·2	32·5	224 37·5	20·6	Suhail	223 14·0	S 43 19·5

32	SUN PLANETS	ARIES	MOON	v or Corrⁿ d	v or Corrⁿ d	v or Corrⁿ d
s	° ′	° ′	° ′	′ ′	′ ′	′ ′
45	8 11·3	8 12·6	7 48·9	4·5 2·4	10·5 5·7	16·5 8·9
46	8 11·5	8 12·8	7 49·1	4·6 2·5	10·6 5·7	16·6 9·0
47	8 11·8	8 13·1	7 49·3	4·7 2·5	10·7 5·8	16·7 9·0
48	8 12·0	8 13·3	7 49·6	4·8 2·6	10·8 5·9	16·8 9·1
49	8 12·3	8 13·6	7 49·8	4·9 2·7	10·9 5·9	16·9 9·2
50	8 12·5	8 13·8	7 50·1	5·0 2·7	11·0 6·0	17·0 9·2
51	8 12·8	8 14·1	7 50·3	5·1 2·8	11·1 6·0	17·1 9·3
52	8 13·0	8 14·3	7 50·5	5·2 2·8	11·2 6·1	17·2 9·3
53	8 13·3	8 14·6	7 50·8	5·3 2·9	11·3 6·1	17·3 9·4
54	8 13·5	8 14·9	7 51·0	5·4 2·9	11·4 6·2	17·4 9·4
55	8 13·8	(8 15·1)	7 51·3	5·5 3·0	11·5 6·2	17·5 9·5
56	8 14·0	8 15·4	7 51·5	5·6 3·0	11·6 6·3	17·6 9·5
57	8 14·3	8 15·6	7 51·7	5·7 3·1	11·7 6·3	17·7 9·6

33	SUN PLANETS	ARIES	MOON	v or Corrⁿ d	v or Corrⁿ d	v or Corrⁿ d
s	° ′	° ′	° ′	′ ′	′ ′	′ ′
45	8 26·3	8 27·6	8 03·2	4·5 2·5	10·5 5·9	16·5 9·2
46	8 26·5	8 27·9	8 03·4	4·6 2·6	10·6 5·9	16·6 9·3
47	8 26·8	(8 28·1)	8 03·7	4·7 2·6	10·7 6·0	16·7 9·3
48	8 27·0	8 28·4	8 03·9	4·8 2·7	10·8 6·0	16·8 9·4
49	8 27·3	8 28·6	8 04·1	4·9 2·7	10·9 6·1	16·9 9·4
50	8 27·5	8 28·9	8 04·4	5·0 2·8	11·0 6·1	17·0 9·5
51	8 27·8	8 29·1	8 04·6	5·1 2·8	11·1 6·2	17·1 9·5
52	8 28·0	8 29·4	8 04·9	5·2 2·9	11·2 6·3	17·2 9·6
53	8 28·3	8 29·6	8 05·1	5·3 3·0	11·3 6·3	17·3 9·7
54	8 28·5	8 29·9	8 05·3	5·4 3·0	11·4 6·4	17·4 9·7
55	8 28·8	8 30·1	8 05·6	5·5 3·1	11·5 6·4	17·5 9·8
56	8 29·0	8 30·4	8 05·8	5·6 3·1	11·6 6·5	17·6 9·8
57	8 29·3	8 30·6	8 06·1	5·7 3·2	11·7 6·5	17·7 9·9

	GHA	Dec
8d 01h	91°39′	
33m 47s	8°28′	
Procyon	245°30′	5°18′N
	345°37′	

A worthwhile shortcut should be noted here. While you have the daily page open, copy down both the GHA Aries figure on the first line, and the Procyon figures on the third line. Then open the tinted section and write down the increment figure on the second line. This saves thumbing back and forth through the Almanac.

One more example will illustrate a case which you will meet frequently. For the star Sirius, on December 8, 1973, GMT 07h 32m 55s:

	GHA	Dec
8d 07h	181°54′	
32m 55s	8°15′	
Sirius	259°00′	16°41′S
	449°09′	
	− 360°00′	
	89°09′	

In this case, the GHA values added up to give a figure greater than 360 degrees, or a whole circle. The cure for this is simply to subtract 360 degrees.

Finding your LOP by a star sight, then, involves measuring hs and applying sextant corrections, finding the GHA and Dec as just shown, and using sight reduction tables to obtain Hc and plot the LOP in the usual way. A complete example is given here.

A vessel at DR position 50°52'N, 22°07'W, takes an evening sight of Arcturus, on June 18, 1973, GMT 22h 57m 04s. The sextant reading is 56°11'. Index error is 06' off the arc; height of eye is 14 feet. The resulting plot of the LOP is shown in Figure 10-2.

		Arcturus hs 56°11'
		IC +06'
		Dip -04'
18d 22h	237°00'	App Alt 56°13'
57m 04s	14°18'	Ref -01'
	146°23' 19°19'N	Ho 56°12'
	397°41'	
	37°41'	
aλ	21°41'W Tab Dec 19° Same	
MA	16°W Tab Hc 55°35' d +57' Z = N153W	
aL	51°N +18' a = 19T	
	Hc 55°53'	

DECLINATION (15°-29°) SAME NAME AS LATITUDE   **LAT 51°**

	15°			16°			17°			18°			19°			20°			21°			22°			23°		
LHA	Hc	d	Z	Hc	d	Z	Hc	d	Z	Hc	d	Z	Hc	d	Z	Hc	d	Z	Hc	d	Z	Hc	d	Z	Hc	d	Z
0	54 00	+60	180	55 00	+60	180	56 00	+60	180	57 00	+60	180	58 00	+60	180	59 00	+60	180	60 00	+60	180	61 00	+60	180	62 00	+60	180
1	54 00	59	178	54 59	60	178	55 59	60	178	56 59	60	178	57 59	60	178	58 59	60	178	59 59	60	178	60 59	60	178	61 59	60	178
2	53 58	60	177	54 58	60	177	55 58	60	177	56 58	60	177	57 58	60	176	58 58	60	176	59 58	60	176	60 58	59	176	61 57	60	176
3	53 55	60	175	54 55	60	175	55 55	60	175	56 55	60	175	57 55	60	175	58 55	60	175	59 55	59	174	60 54	60	174	61 54	60	174
4	53 51	60	173	54 51	60	173	55 51	60	173	56 51	60	173	57 51	59	173	58 50	60	173	59 50	60	173	60 50	60	172	61 50	59	172
5	53 47	+59	172	54 46	+60	172	55 46	+60	172	56 46	+59	171	57 45	+60	171	58 45	+60	171	59 45	+59	171	60 44	+60	171	61 44	+60	176
6	53 41	59	170	54 40	60	170	55 40	59	170	56 39	60	170	57 39	60	169	58 39	59	169	59 38	60	169	60 38	59	169	61 37	59	168
7	53 34	59	169	54 33	60	168	55 33	59	168	56 32	59	168	57 31	60	168	58 31	59	167	59 30	59	167	60 29	59	167	61 29	59	166
8	53 26	59	167	54 25	59	167	55 24	60	166	56 24	59	166	57 23	59	166	58 22	59	166	59 21	59	165	60 20	59	165	61 19	59	165
9	53 17	59	165	54 16	59	165	55 15	59	165	56 14	59	165	57 13	59	164	58 12	59	164	59 11	59	163	60 10	59	163	61 09	58	163
10	53 07	+59	164	54 06	+59	164	55 05	+58	163	56 03	+59	163	57 02	+59	162	58 01	+59	162	59 00	+58	162	59 58	+59	161	60 57	+58	161
11	52 56	58	162	53 54	59	162	54 53	59	162	55 52	58	161	56 50	59	161	57 49	58	160	58 47	58	160	59 45	59	159	60 44	58	159
12	52 44	58	161	53 42	59	160	54 41	58	160	55 39	58	160	56 37	59	159	57 36	58	159	58 34	58	158	59 32	58	158	60 30	57	157
13	52 31	58	159	53 29	58	159	54 27	58	158	55 25	58	158	56 23	58	157	57 21	58	157	58 19	58	156	59 17	57	156	60 14	58	155
14	52 17	58	158	53 15	58	157	54 13	58	157	55 11	57	156	56 08	58	156	57 06	57	155	58 03	58	155	59 01	57	154	59 58	57	154
15	52 02	+58	156	53 00	+57	156	53 57	+58	155	54 55	+57	155	55 52	+58	154	56 50	+57	154	57 47	+57	153	58 44	+57	153	59 41	+56	152
16	51 46	57	155	52 43	58	154	53 41	57	154	54 38	57	153	55 35	57	153	56 32	57	152	57 29	57	151	58 26	56	151	59 22	57	150
17	51 29	57	153	52 26	58	153	53 24	57	152	54 21	56	152	55 17	57	151	56 14	57	150	57 11	56	150	58 07	56	149	59 03	56	148
18	51 12	57	152	52 09	56	151	53 05	57	151	54 02	57	150	54 59	56	149	55 55	56	149	56 51	56	148	57 47	56	148	58 43	55	147
19	50 53	57	150	51 50	56	150	52 46	57	149	53 43	56	149	54 39	56	148	55 35	56	147	56 31	55	147	57 26	56	146	58 22	55	145

A few words are in order concerning the selection of stars to use for sights. First of all, star sights, like planet sights, are usually done at twilight when the horizon is visible. This means that you will want to use a bright star, preferably magnitude 2.0 or brighter. The daily page listing doesn't give magnitude, but the list on the next-to-last page of the Almanac does. Remember that a magnitude 1.2 star (Pollux) is brighter than a magnitude 1.8 star (Alnilam), and that a magnitude –1.6 star (Sirius) is brightest of all.

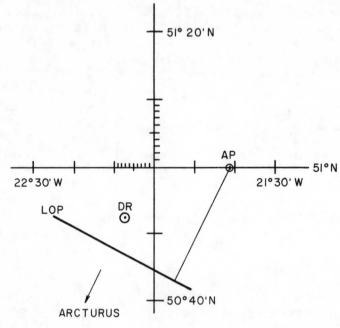

Figure 10-2.

Second, it's desirable to use stars whose altitudes at the time of sight-ing are between 10° and 70°. At very low altitudes, refraction correc-tions become large and somewhat variable. At very high altitudes, the approximation we make by drawing a straight LOP becomes a poor one, introducing possible errors.

Third, since HO 249 covers a Dec range only between 29°S and 29°N, not all the stars in the selected list are usable. This isn't a big problem, though, since 29 of the 57 stars are within this range, and those 29 stars include most of the popular ones. The sun, moon, and planets are also within this declination range. If a person really insists on using stars with declination greater than 29°, he can do so by using one of the other sight reduction tables. These are covered in Chapter 11.

Finally, you'll want to choose stars which lie in different directions, so the LOP's will cross at a good angle. Ideally, three stars should be used, spaced about equally. The LOP's will then intersect at angles, similar to the plotting practice problem of Chapter 9, as shown in the Appendix. If they don't intersect exactly, they will form a small triangle, and the center is taken as the fix.

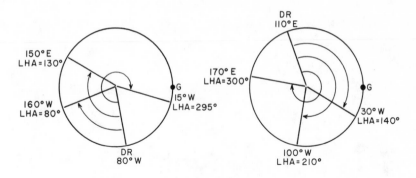

Figure 10-3.

LATITUDE BY POLARIS

Since the measured altitude of Polaris gives very nearly the latitude of the observer, the exact latitude may be obtained quite easily by adding a couple of correction factors. These allow for the fact the Polaris is not located exactly at the celestial pole. The Table of Corrections is just in front of the tinted "Increments and Corrections" section of the Almanac. Use of the table is very simple and is illustrated with an example, so I won't deal with it beyond explaining a new term you will find used.

That term is LHA Aries, meaning the local hour angle of Aries. This is the difference between the assumed longitude (aλ) and the GHA of Aries, measured *westward through 360 degrees.* The GHA of Aries is looked up in the same way as usual. The calculation of the LHA is illustrated in Figure 10-3.

Here is a practice problem. Answer to be found in the Appendix.

4. Find the GHA and declination of the star Arcturus on June 19, 1973, GMT 01h 57m 04s.

11 Other Sight Reduction Tables

Instruments have been improved, tables have been made more complete and simpler to use, yet the tools and techniques are essentially those of two centuries ago.

Carleton Mitchell, *Passage East*

Throughout this book, HO 249 sight reduction tables have been used. The reason for this preference, as explained in Chapter 7, is that these tables are cheaper, more compact, and easier to use than other types. However, three other types of tables are in current use. These are HO 211, HO 214, and HO 229. These tables all serve exactly the same function; that is, they enable you to determine the calculated altitude (Hc), and the azimuth angle (Z). The details of using the tables differ slightly, though. Each table has strong and weak points. This chapter explains the use of each type. As an aid to comparison, the same example situation is worked out with each type of table.

The situation is this: A navigator whose DR position is 41°15′N, 127°51′W takes a sight. After applying the usual sextant corrections, he finds that Ho = 62°50′. With the Almanac, he finds that at the time of the sight, the body's GHA was 143°20′, and the declination was 17°14′N.

HO 214

This is the classic sight reduction table used for many years in the navy. A complete set of tables fills nine volumes, each covering 10 degrees of latitude. Most of the volumes are reprinted every few years, and the prices vary somewhat, but a complete set will cost about $45. The set is about 4 times bulkier and heavier than HO 249. There are two distinct differences. First, the range of declination covers the sun, moon, planets, and all the 57 navigational stars, but only those stars. For example, since there is no navigational star at a Dec of 57°, that value is not listed. Second, the values of Hc are tabulated with an accuracy of 0'.1. This isn't a great advantage to the navigator, since other sources of error are usually much greater. However, if you have a really accurate sextant and catch the accuracy bug, you may appreciate this feature.

To solve the example problem, you proceed very much as with HO 249. The assumed latitude (aL) is chosen as a whole degree; 41°N. The assumed longitude (aλ) is chosen to give a whole degree of MA. In this case an aλ of 128°20′W gives an MA of 15°W. The next smaller tabulated value of Dec (17°) is used. A portion of the appropriate page (Vol. V, p. 36) is extracted below. Notice that the page is identified by Latitude and Declination Same Name as Latitude, as in HO 249, but the column headings are different. Alt. replaces Hc, Δd replaces d, and Az. replaces Z. The MA is here called hour angle (H.A.).

DECLINATION SAME NAME AS LATITUDE

Lat. 41°	H.A.	16° 00′ Alt.	Δd Δt	Az.	16° 30′ Alt.	Δd Δt	Az.	17° 00′ Alt.	Δd Δt	Az.	17° 30′ Alt.	Δd Δt	Az.	18° 00′ Alt.	Δd Δt	Az.	18° 30′ Alt.	Δd Δt	Az.	Dec
	00	65 00.0	1.0 02	180.0	65 30.0	1.0 02	180.0	66 00.0	1.0 02	180.0	66 30.0	1.0 02	180.0	67 00.0	1.0 02	180.0	67 30.0	1.0 02	180.0	
	1	64 59.1	1.0 04	177.7	65 29.1	1.0 05	177.7	65 59.1	1.0 05	177.6	66 29.1	1.0 05	177.6	66 59.0	1.0 05	177.6	67 29.0	1.0 05	177.5	
	2	64 56.4	1.0 07	175.5	65 26.4	1.0 08	175.4	65 56.3	1.0 08	175.3	66 26.2	1.0 08	175.2	66 56.2	1.0 08	175.1	67 26.1	1.0 08	175.1	
	3	64 51.9	1.0 10	173.2	65 21.8	1.0 11	173.1	65 51.7	1.0 11	173.0	66 21.5	1.0 11	172.8	66 51.4	99 11	172.7	67 21.2	99 11	172.6	
	4	64 45.7	99 13	171.0	65 15.5	99 14	170.8	65 45.2	99 14	170.7	66 15.0	99 14	170.5	66 44.7	99 14	170.3	67 14.4	99 14	170.2	
	05	64 37.7	99 16	168.7	65 07.3	99 16	168.5	65 37.0	99 17	168.4	66 06.6	99 17	168.2	66 36.2	99 17	168.0	67 05.7	99 18	167.7	
	6	64 28.0	98 19	166.5	64 57.5	98 19	166.3	65 26.9	98 20	166.1	65 56.4	98 20	165.8	66 25.8	98 20	165.6	66 55.2	98 21	165.4	
	7	64 16.6	98 22	164.3	64 45.9	98 22	164.1	65 15.2	98 22	163.8	65 44.4	97 23	163.6	66 13.7	97 23	163.3	66 42.9	97 24	163.0	
	8	64 03.6	97 24	162.2	64 32.7	97 25	161.9	65 01.7	97 25	161.6	65 30.8	97 26	161.3	65 59.8	97 26	161.0	66 28.7	96 26	160.7	
	9	63 48.9	96 27	160.1	64 17.8	96 27	159.8	64 46.6	96 28	159.4	65 15.5	96 28	159.1	65 44.2	96 29	158.8	66 12.9	96 29	158.4	
	10	63 32.7	96 30	158.0	64 01.4	95 30	157.7	64 30.0	95 30	157.3	64 58.5	95 31	157.0	65 27.0	95 31	156.6	65 55.4	95 32	156.2	
	1	63 15.0	95 32	156.0	63 43.4	95 32	155.6	64 11.7	94 33	155.2	64 40.0	94 33	154.8	65 08.2	94 34	154.4	65 36.4	94 34	154.0	
	2	62 55.8	94 34	153.9	63 24.0	94 35	153.6	63 52.0	93 35	153.2	64 20.0	93 36	152.8	64 47.9	93 36	152.3	65 15.8	93 37	151.9	
	3	62 35.2	93 37	152.0	63 03.1	93 37	151.6	63 30.9	92 38	151.2	63 58.6	92 38	150.7	64 26.2	92 39	150.3	64 53.7	92 39	149.8	
	4	62 13.3	92 39	150.1	62 40.9	92 39	149.6	63 08.4	91 40	149.2	63 35.8	91 40	148.7	64 03.1	91 41	148.3	64 30.3	91 41	147.8	
	15	61 50.1	91 41	148.2	62 17.3	91 41	147.7	62 44.5	90 42	147.3	63 11.6	90 42	146.8	63 38.6	90 43	146.3	64 05.5	89 43	145.8	
	6	61 25.6	90 43	146.4	61 52.6	90 43	145.9	62 19.4	89 44	145.4	62 46.2	89 44	144.9	63 12.9	89 45	144.4	63 39.4	88 45	143.9	
	7	60 59.9	89 45	144.6	61 26.6	89 45	144.1	61 53.1	88 46	143.6	62 19.6	88 46	143.1	62 45.9	88 47	142.6	63 12.2	87 47	142.0	
	8	60 33.1	88 46	142.8	60 59.5	88 47	142.3	61 25.7	87 48	141.8	61 51.8	87 48	141.3	62 17.9	87 49	140.8	62 43.7	86 49	140.2	
	9	60 05.2	87 48	141.1	60 31.3	87 49	140.6	60 57.2	86 49	140.1	61 23.0	86 50	139.6	61 48.7	85 50	139.0	62 14.3	85 51	138.5	

Alt. and Az. are equivilent to Hc and Z of HO 249, but Δd is different from d. In HO 249, the d value is the number of minutes of altitude difference between successive Dec values, and has to be proportioned, or *interpolated,* according to the excess minutes of Dec, i.e., the difference in values between the tabulated and the actual figure. However, in HO 214, the $\Delta\,d$ value represents the altitude difference divided by 60. Accordingly, the $\Delta\,d$ value must be *multiplied* by the excess minutes of declination. A slide rule is handy for this; you can also use the multiplication table on the inside back cover. Also note that the $\Delta\,d$ figure of 90 has an implied decimal, so it must be written .90, and the sign must be determined by inspection. In this case, the Alt. value for declination 17°30′ is *greater* than the Alt. value for declination 17°00′, so $\Delta\,d$ is *positive.* Putting it all together, the work looks like this:

GHA 143°20′	Dec 17°14′N	Ho = 62°50′.0
aλ 128°20′W	Tab Dec 17°00′ Same	
MA 15°W	Alt. 62°44′.5	Δd +.90 Az. N147W
aL 41°N	corr'n +12′.6	
	Hc 62°57′.1	a = 7.1A

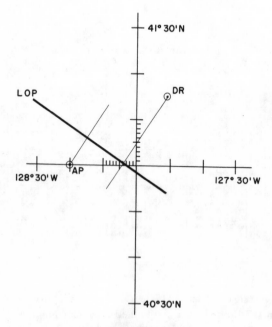

Figure 11-1.

Notice that Az. is rounded to the nearest degree, and has the N-S prefix and E-W suffix attached in the same way as HO 249. The value of *a* is worked out and the LOP is plotted in the usual way. The result is shown in Figure 11-1.

HO 229

This is a recent publication, basically similar to HO 214. Six volumes, each covering 15° of latitude, make up the complete set. The total size, weight, and cost is similar to HO 214. An interesting feature of this series is that the entire calculation and preparation of the printing plates was done by computer. This presumably means that no printing errors are present, in contrast with HO 214, which had several errors in the early printings of most of the volumes.

There are two basic differences from HO 214. First, *all* values of Dec are listed. Second, the pages are arranged in order of local hour angle (LHA), rather than latitude. Take note: LHA is measured from the AP always westward to the GP, through 360°. Accordingly, an MA of 15°W equals an LHA of 15°, while an MA of 15°E equals an LHA of 345°. The same page applies to both LHA's, though, so both figures are listed at the page heading. You can continue thinking in terms of MA by just using the first figure of the LHA page heading. This system has the advantage of eliminating the conversion of Azimuth Angle (Z) into Azimuth (Zn), and is consistent with the method of using all the other tables.

15°, 345° L.H.A.   LATITUDE SAME NAME AS DECLINATION

Dec.	38° Hc	d	Z	39° Hc	d	Z	40° Hc	d	Z	41° Hc	d	Z	42° Hc	d	Z	43° Hc	d	Z	Lat.
0	49 34.0	+56.9	156.5	48 38.9	+57.1	156.9	47 43.6	+57.3	157.4	46 48.1	+57.5	157.8	45 52.5	+57.6	158.2	44 56.7	+57.8	158.6	
1	50 30.9	56.8	156.0	49 36.0	57.0	156.5	48 40.9	57.1	156.9	47 45.6	57.3	157.4	46 50.1	57.6	157.8	45 54.5	57.7	158.2	
2	51 27.7	56.6	155.5	50 33.0	56.8	156.0	49 38.0	57.1	156.5	48 42.9	57.3	156.9	47 47.7	57.4	157.4	46 52.2	57.6	157.8	
3	52 24.3	56.4	154.9	51 29.8	56.7	155.5	50 35.1	56.9	156.0	49 40.2	57.1	156.5	48 45.1	57.3	156.9	47 49.8	57.5	157.4	
4	53 20.7	56.3	154.4	52 26.5	56.6	154.9	51 32.0	56.8	155.5	50 37.3	57.1	156.0	49 42.4	57.3	156.5	48 47.3	57.4	156.9	
5	54 17.0	+56.2	153.8	53 23.1	+56.4	154.4	52 28.8	+56.7	155.0	51 34.4	+56.9	155.5	50 39.7	+57.1	156.0	49 44.7	+57.3	156.5	
6	55 13.2	55.9	153.2	54 19.5	56.2	153.8	53 25.5	56.5	154.4	52 31.3	56.7	155.0	51 36.8	57.0	155.5	50 42.1	57.2	156.0	
7	56 09.1	55.7	152.5	55 15.7	56.1	153.2	54 22.0	56.3	153.8	53 28.0	56.6	154.4	52 33.8	56.8	155.0	51 39.3	57.0	155.5	
8	57 04.8	55.5	151.9	56 11.8	55.8	152.6	55 18.3	56.2	153.2	54 24.6	56.4	153.9	53 30.6	56.7	154.5	52 36.3	57.0	155.0	
9	58 00.3	55.3	151.2	57 07.6	55.6	151.9	56 14.5	55.9	152.6	55 21.0	56.3	153.3	54 27.3	56.5	153.9	53 33.3	56.8	154.5	
10	58 55.6	+55.0	150.4	58 03.2	+55.4	151.2	57 10.4	+55.8	152.0	56 17.3	+56.1	152.7	55 23.8	+56.4	153.3	54 30.1	+56.6	154.0	
11	59 50.6	54.6	149.6	58 58.6	55.1	150.5	58 06.2	55.5	151.3	57 13.4	55.8	152.0	56 20.2	56.2	152.7	55 26.7	56.5	153.4	
12	60 45.2	54.4	148.8	59 53.7	54.8	149.7	59 01.7	55.2	150.5	58 09.2	55.6	151.3	57 16.4	56.0	152.1	56 23.2	56.3	152.8	
13	61 39.6	54.0	147.9	60 48.5	54.5	148.9	59 56.9	54.9	149.8	59 04.8	55.4	150.6	58 12.4	55.7	151.4	57 19.5	56.1	152.2	
14	62 33.6	53.6	147.0	61 43.0	54.1	148.0	60 51.8	54.7	148.9	60 00.2	55.1	149.8	59 08.1	55.5	150.7	58 15.6	55.8	151.5	
15	63 27.2	+53.1	146.0	62 37.1	+53.8	147.1	61 46.5	+54.3	148.1	60 55.3	+54.8	149.0	60 03.6	+55.2	149.9	59 11.4	+55.7	150.8	
16	64 20.3	52.7	144.9	63 30.9	53.3	146.1	62 40.8	53.9	147.2	61 50.1	54.4	148.2	60 58.8	54.9	149.1	60 07.1	55.3	150.0	
17	65 13.0	52.2	143.8	64 24.2	52.9	145.0	63 34.7	53.5	146.2	62 44.5	54.1	147.3	61 53.7	54.6	148.3	61 02.4	55.1	149.3	
18	66 05.2	51.5	142.6	65 17.1	52.3	143.9	64 28.2	53.0	145.2	63 38.6	53.7	146.3	62 48.3	54.3	147.4	61 57.5	54.8	148.4	
19	66 56.7	50.9	141.3	66 09.4	51.7	142.7	65 21.2	52.5	144.1	64 32.3	53.2	145.3	63 42.6	53.8	146.5	62 52.3	54.4	147.5	

For the example problem, the assumed latitude and assumed longitude (aL and aλ) are worked as before. We then have an MA of 15°W, so we use the LHA 15° page (Vol. 3, p. 214). An extract of this page is given here. Notice that the column headings – Hc, d, and Z – are the same as in HO 249. They also have the same meanings. The tabulated declinations are listed down the side.

Using the tabulated Dec value of 17°, extract the values of Hc, d, and Z. Both the decimal and sign of d are shown, not implied. The value of d must be *interpolated* according to the excess minutes of declination, as in HO 249. A table for this purpose is included on the front and back inside covers. It's more accurate than corresponding Table 5 in HO 249, and accordingly more cumbersome to use. Examples of the method of using the table are given in the Introduction to each volume. The work is arranged as shown.

GHA 143°20′	Dec 17°14′ N		Ho 62°50′.0
aλ 128°20′W	Tab Dec 17° Same		
MA 15°W	Tab Hc 62°44′.5		d +54′.1 Z = N147W
aL 51°N	+11′.6		
	+ 1′.0		
	Hc 62°57′.1		a = 7.1A

Here the correction to the tabulated Hc is applied in two steps. The result is the same as we obtained from HO 214, so the LOP plot is exactly the same line in Figure 11-1. Since the result is the same, you may wonder what advantage these tables offer. First, there is the complete range of Dec, which may be helpful if you're using a star other than one of the standard 57. There are also applications to other problems, such as great-circle calculations. These applications are explained in the Introduction. Second, the tables are more accurate. Although they are tabulated to the same 0′.1 as HO 214, the method of calculating the values has been improved, so that some values listed in HO 229 are more accurate than the corresponding values in HO 214. In addition, the method of interpolating the excess minutes of declination is more accurate, and further refinements for obtaining maximum accuracy in special situations are given in the tables.

For the average navigator, accuracy of this order is unwarranted. It's pointless to compute Hc to a tenth of a minute accuracy, and then compare it with a sextant observation of only a couple of minutes accuracy. This means that the only practical advantage of HO 229 or HO 214 is in the occasional situation where you must observe a star whose Dec is outside the range of HO 249. For these few situations, a much more practical alternative is offered by HO 211, as explained below.

HO 211

This is a different kettle of fish altogether. The size is right — one compact volume does it all. The price is also right — 90 cents if you're lucky, $1.50 if you're not. The catch? It's not quite so handy to use. But you won't use it often, and at that price, who's fussy? It also has an advantage that none of the other tables offer. Read on!

The HO 211 was published for a long time by the Hydrographic Office, and was standard equipment for lifeboats. It has now been discontinued, but a lot of copies are still around — at the original price of 90 cents. If you can't find one of these, you can buy a reprint published by Carlsen and Larsen, of Seattle, Washington. It's distributed by Weems and Plath, of Annapolis, Maryland, at the price of $1.50. You should have a copy or two. Keep one at home and leave one on the boat.

Now, what about using it? Basically, you add and subtract a bunch of numbers from two columns labeled A and B. At the end of the arithmetic, you get the values of Hc and Z, which are used in the normal way to plot the LOP. The table has an introduction, with worked examples, but some comments about the examples are in order.

First of all, when this table was published, the system of timekeeping and the arrangement of the Almanac was much different from that used today. The first ten lines of problem 1 on page 7 are in terms of GCT (Greenwich Civil Time), Eq T (equation of time), RA (right ascension), and won't mean much to you. Ignore them. Work out the GHA and Dec of the body you've observed in the usual way, and start reading on the eleventh line — GHA:arc. Second, an important feature of HO 211 is that you don't have to use an assumed position which gives latitude and meridian angle in whole degrees, as you do with all the other tables. Use your DR position, and let the latitude and MA come out as they will. Here you will encounter a discrepancy in nomenclature. The meridian angle is measured and used in HO 211 just as in the other tables, but here it is misnamed LHA. The key to its real identity is that it is always shown with the E-W suffix.

With regard to our example problem, we will use the DR latitude of $41°15'$N. The DR longitude of $127°51'$W, combined with the GHA of $143°20'$, gives a meridian angle of $15°29'$W. The Dec will be taken at its actual value of $17°14'$N.

```
GHA  143°20'
DR λ 127°51'W        Add              Sub              Add              Sub
MA    15°29'W    +A 57356
Dec   17°14'N      B  1995        _A 52832
                   A 59351         B  1460        B 1460           A 59351
K     17°50'.5N◄ ─ ─ ─ ─ ─ ─A 51372
DRL   41°15'.0N                              +
K∼L   23°24'.5 ─ ─ ─ ─ ─ ─ ─ ─ ─ ─ ─►  B 3730        ─
Hc    62°32'.5 ◄─ ─ ─ ─ ─ ─ ─ ─ ─ ─ A 5190                   B 33620
Z     N146°W  ◄─ ─ ─ ─ ─ ─ ─ ─ ─ ─ ─ ─ ─ ─ ─ A 25731
Ho    62°50'.0            a = 17.5T
```

Some notes: The values of K and Z may be taken from either the top or the bottom of the pages, according to the size of the angle. The rules for this are given on each page, but be careful not to use the right-hand minute column when using values from the top of the page. The K and L (DRL) may be added or subtracted, depending on whether they have the same or contrary names. Item 9 on page 6 explains this. The Z is named and used in the same way as always. Don't bother converting to Zn. Finally, the Hc and Ho shown on page 7 could easily be misread, due to the small print.

You'll notice that the value of Z obtained (N146W) is about the same as with the other tables, but the value of a (17.5T) is much different from the 7.1A of the previous solutions. This does not indicate an error. Remember that these calculations were based on the DR position, and so the LOP must be plotted from the DR position. When this is done, as shown in Figure 11-1, the LOP turns out to be exactly the same as that obtained by the other solutions.

Plotting from the DR position can be very convenient. If you're using a large-scale chart (one that shows a small area in fine detail), it may not include a whole degree of latitude. In such a case, plotting an LOP calculated from an assumed latitude is a bit tricky, but an LOP calculated from your DR latitude plots very nicely.

Here is a practice problem. Answer to be found in the Appendix.

1. For   aL   41°N
         MA   13°E
         Dec 18°12'N

Find Hc and Z (Az) using HO 214.

12　Portable Calculators

In his ignorance he was not aware . . . that uneducated skippers since navigation began have cheerfully adopted new instruments and techniques at the drop of a hat.

F. Pohl, C. Kornbluth, *Search the Sky*

Today's portable calculators are marvelous things. I use one constantly, and wouldn't be without it. Taking one to sea, though, is another matter altogether. Each person will have his own feelings on the subject; mine are that day-to-day life has complications enough. When I go to sea, I like to leave the frills at home, and trim equipment to the simple basics. The less you take, the less you have to maintain, and the more you enjoy the cruise. For example, I prefer a lead line to a depth sounder every time. There's nothing to go wrong with it. Likewise, a calculator will never replace sight reduction tables on any boat of mine. Calculators will have their applications, though, especially where speed is essential. This chapter is for the man who wants to use one.

There are a tremendous number of models on the market, and new ones are appearing almost daily, so it's not possible to be very specific here about specifications and prices. There are a few general guidelines that may be helpful.

In the matter of operating power, there are three combinations around:

1. Penlight cells only — these tend to get expensive.

2. Penlight cells or AC adapter.

3. Rechargeable nickle-cadmium (NiCad) batteries with an AC adapter which operates the calculator while charging the cells for another stint away from AC power.

This last is probably the most practical rig for use afloat, but it must be remembered that the battery life between recharges isn't very long. About 5 hours of steady use can be expected, though this can be extended by turning the machine off when not using it. If you're going on a longer cruise, you'll need some source of AC power to recharge the batteries. Alternatively, it is possible to build an adapter to run the calculator directly from 12 volts DC, or whatever system your boat might have. You want to know your business to do this. It wouldn't be hard to "pop" the circuit, and the warranty wouldn't apply.

The available features span the entire spectrum, but calculators can be roughly grouped into three categories. There are the so-called "four-function" machines, selling in the $50 range and found absolutely everywhere. Next come the "scientific" machines, with many more functions and a price tag around $200. A few brands dominate the market at this level. Finally, there are programmable calculators, selling for $400 and up. These are very specialized machines, and great fun to use. At the price, they'll find use by only the most dedicated professional navigator, and as such they're beyond the scope of this book.

FOUR-FUNCTION CALCULATORS

These are far and away the most popular machines. There are so many makes and models that it's not feasible or necessary to single out any particular one. Their features have a great deal in common. They all have the four common functions (+ - X ÷), and some have a % key as well. There may be other functions such as the reciprocal (1/X), and there may be a way of storing a constant, which is very handy. Some of these machines will do "chain" calculations and some won't. Each type has its own operating rules, and there are enough differences between them that I won't offer any specific guidelines here. Read your manual.

The application of four-function calculators falls into three broad categories:

1. Speed-time-distance problems; not strictly part of celestial navigation, but useful.
2. Addition, subtraction, and averaging of time and angles.
3. Corrections to the tabulated value of Hc in sight reduction tables.

Speed-Time-Distance

All this work is based on the formula $D = S \times T$; the distance in nautical miles equals the speed in knots times the time in hours. The two variants of the formula are also used; $S = D/T$ and $T = D/S$.

Example 1: What distance will you cover in 5 hours at 4.5 knots?

$$D = 4.5 \times 5 = 22.5 \text{ miles}$$

Example 2: What time is required to travel 121 miles at an average of 5.5 knots?

$$T = \frac{121}{5.5} = 22 \text{ hours}$$

Example 3: You travel 23.5 miles in 5 hours. What was your speed?

$$S = \frac{23.5}{5} = 4.7 \text{ knots}$$

In the above examples, the times were whole numbers of hours. If the time is given in hours and minutes, you must convert to hours and decimals before working the problem. If the answer to a problem comes out in hours and decimals, you have to convert to hours and minutes.

Example 4: Your speed is 7 knots. How far will you travel in 3 hours 24 minutes?

$$\frac{24m}{60m} = .4h \qquad\qquad D = 7 \times 3.4 = 23.8 \text{ miles}$$

Example 5: What time is required to travel 56.7 miles at 4.5 knots?

$$T = \frac{56.7}{4.5} = 12.6h$$

$$.6h \times 60 = 36m \qquad\qquad Time = 12h\ 36m$$

Times

Because our time system works on a base of 60 rather than 10, times given in hours and minutes can't be added or subtracted like other numbers. There are several "gimmicks" you can use, though. On a four-function machine, the simplest way is to insert dummy zeros into the figures. Thus 12 hours 26 minutes (12h 26m) becomes 12026. In this form, the numbers can be added or subtracted, the zero serving effectively as a buffer between units.

Example 6: Add 8m 31s to 23m 14s

```
   23014
+   8031
   31045
Ans. 31m 45s
```

Example 7: Subtract 5m 18s from 31m 25s

```
   31025
−   5018
   26007
Ans. 26m 07s
```

Example 8: Add 2h 11m 05s to 12h 27m 48s

```
  12027048
+  2011005
  14038053
Ans. 14h 38m 53s
```

In the examples above, the answers came out with no unit more than 60, and so were ready to use. If any unit comes out greater than 60, *that unit* must be modified by adding or subtracting 940, depending on whether the original problem was addition or subtraction.

Example 9: Add 11m 52s to 47m 34s

```
   47034
+  11052
   58086
+    940
   59026
Ans. 59m 26s
```

Example 10: Subtract 4m 53s from 10m 41s

```
   10041
−   4053
    5988
−    940
    5048
Ans. 5m 48s
```

Example 11: Add 1h 45m 10s to 14h 57m 35s

```
  14057035
+  1045010
  15102045
+   940000
  16042045
Ans. 16h 42m 45s
```

Example 12: Subtract 2h 45m 33s from 6h 21m 17s

$$\begin{array}{r} 6021017 \\ - \; \underline{2045033} \\ 3975984 \\ - \; \underline{\;940940} \\ 3035044 \\ \textit{Ans. 3h 35m 44s} \end{array}$$

Angles

Angles, like time, are measured in a base 60 system. We divide degrees into 60 minutes, and minutes into 60 seconds. The system just described for adding or subtracting times also works for angle calculations. The following two examples are in the familiar degree-minute system.

Example 13: Add 59°14′ to 45°27′

$$\begin{array}{r} 45027 \\ + \; \underline{59014} \\ 104041 \\ \textit{Ans. 104°41′} \end{array}$$

Example 14: Subtract 5°42′ from 63°18′

$$\begin{array}{r} 63018 \\ - \; \underline{\;5042} \\ 57976 \\ - \; \underline{\;\;940} \\ 57036 \\ \textit{Ans. 57°36′} \end{array}$$

When more precision is desired in navigation work, the angles are often given in degrees, minutes, and tenths of minutes. The *Nautical Almanac,* HO214, and HO229 all use this system. Angles to tenths of minutes can be handled using the same basic method of buffer zeros, modified slightly. You can add an extra digit with the decimal point interspersed, or you can add the extra digit with an imaginary decimal point.

Example 15: Add 5°15′.8 to 27°14′.7

$$\begin{array}{r} 27014.7 \\ + \; \underline{5015.8} \\ 32030.5 \\ \textit{Ans. 32°30′.5} \end{array}$$

Example 16: Subtract 11°25′.9 from 93°32′.4

$$\begin{array}{r} 930324 \\ - \; \underline{110259} \\ 820065 \\ \textit{Ans. 82°06′.5} \end{array}$$

Example 17: Add 22°25′.1 to 64°35′.7

$$
\begin{array}{r}
640357 \\
+\ \underline{220251} \\
860608 \\
+\ \underline{\ \ 9400} \\
870008 \\
Ans.\ 87°00'.8
\end{array}
$$

Example 18: Subtract 24°42′.7 from 38°08′.0

$$
\begin{array}{r}
38008.0 \\
-\ \underline{24042.7} \\
13965.3 \\
-\ \underline{\ \ 940.0} \\
13025.3 \\
Ans.\ 13°25'.3
\end{array}
$$

In astronomical and survey work, and occasionally in navigation, angles are expressed in degrees, minutes, and seconds. These can be handled just like times in hours, minutes, and seconds.

Example 19: Add 2°41′15″ to 16°34′28″

$$
\begin{array}{r}
16034028 \\
+\ \underline{2041015} \\
18075043 \\
+\ \underline{\ 940000} \\
19015043 \\
Ans.\ 19°15'43''
\end{array}
$$

Occasionally you may want to find the average of a number of times or angles. One application is taking sights, where you can take several sights at short intervals and average the results to reduce the individual uncertainties. On a four-function calculator, the procedure is to add the individual times in minutes and seconds using the method already shown, then convert the total to decimal units, then divide by the number of readings, and finally convert the answer back to minutes and seconds.

Example 20: Find the average time for sights taken at 18h 22m 17s
18h 23m 05s
18h 23m 51s
18h 25m 12s

Since all the times are at 18h, we can omit that figure from the work and replace it at the end. The work shown on page 115 is done on a typical calculator, but the details may vary from machine to machine.

KEY	DISPLAY	COMMENT
22017		
+ 23005		
+ 23051		
+ 25012		
=	93085	
+ 940		
=	94025	Total time 94m 25s, write down
25		
÷ 60		
=	.41	
+ 94		
=	94.41	Total time
÷ 4		
=	23.60	Average time, write 23m
− 23		
=	.60	
x 60		
=	36.25	Round to 36s Answer 18h 23m 36s

Corrections to Tabulated Hc

When you enter sight reduction tables to find the values of Hc and Z, you use a whole degree of Declination. The tables give a correction factor to allow for the "excess Dec" — the difference between the actual value and the tabulated value. This correction factor is called "d" in HO 229 and HO 249 tables, and "Δd" in HO 214 tables. Depending on which type of table you are using, calculating the correction is either a multiplication or an interpolation. It can be done with the auxiliary table provided at the front or back of the sight reduction tables; it can also be done very nicely on a calculator.

Example 21: The example sun-sight at the front of this book has an excess Dec of 05′. From HO 249 tables, d = +51′. The correction is found by using 51′ as a fraction of 60′, and then multiplying by 05′, i.e.,

$$\frac{51'}{60'} \times 05'$$

KEY	DISPLAY	COMMENT
51		
÷60		
x 5		
=	4.25	Correction is + 04'

Example 22: The example star sight at the back of this book has an excess Dec of 48', and *d* from the HO 249 tables is –52'. The calculation to be done is

$$\frac{-52'}{60'} \times 48'$$

KEY	DISPLAY	COMMENT
52		
+/–		
÷60		
x 48		
=	–41.6	Correction is –42'

We can continue by adding 30°09 to get the value of Hc.

+ 30009.0		
=	29967.4	
–940.0		
=	29027.4	Hc is 29°27'

Notice here that the 940.0 must be subtracted, rather than added as you might first think. The reason is that the previous step is in fact the subtraction of 41.6 from 30009.0, and we must follow with another subtraction.

The method of using $\triangle d$ from the HO 214 tables is slightly different. In this case, you just multiply the value of $\triangle d$ by the excess Dec.

Example 23: The sight worked out on page 104 has an excess Dec of 14'. The tabulated Hc is 62°44'.5, and $\triangle d$ = +.90.

.90		
x14		
=	12.6	Correction is 12'.6

We can now add the tabulated Hc to obtain the actual Hc.

+ 62044.5		
=	62057.1	$Hc = 62°57'.1$

Note that this agrees exactly with Hc as worked out by the correction table method.

SCIENTIFIC CALCULATORS

The most obvious distinguishing feature of these machines is the addition of trigonometry functions — sin, cos, and tan. They also have a memory for storing a constant, and several working registers for holding intermediate results. Other features are included, such as logs, factorials, and powers, but these are less important in navigation work. At the moment, the two usual models are Hewlett-Packard's HP-35, and Texas Instruments' SR-50. They appear nearly identical, cost about $200, and operate from AC or from rechargeable NiCad batteries. Change is rampant in this class of machine, however. Both companies are bringing out new models at lower prices, and other companies are entering the field.

The scientific calculators can do any of the problems already shown. In addition, their extra features allow a great range of additional work. The registers and memory make time and angle calculations more straightforward. The trig functions allow the solution of the navigational triangle directly, so that sight reduction tables are not required. The trig functions also apply nicely to a whole pile of coastwise piloting work, but that subject is beyond the scope of this book.

There are two different systems of problem solution available to calculator makers, and currently they are both in use. One system, typified by the SR-50, is basically the same as used on the four-function machines. There is an = key, which is used at various stages of the problem. For those readers familiar with algebra, the = key serves approximately the same function as the right hand parenthesis in a nested expression. The other system, used on all HP machines and others as well, is known as Reverse Polish Notation (honest!), or RPN. On these machines, there is no = key, but instead an ENTER (↑) key serves about the same function as the left hand parenthesis of a nested expression.

Each of these systems has its backers, and there is a minor war going on about their relative advantages and otherwise. TI claims that the = key is simpler; HP counters that RPN is more consistent and faster.

My own vote goes to the RPN system, which is quickly learned and un-questionably shorter for the more complex problems. The results of intermediate steps are displayed automatically, which is very helpful.

The rest of the examples in this chapter illustrate the use of both the HP35 and the SR50 as representative types. Where the HP35 is used, ↑ represents the ENTER key. The keystroke sequences given are not necessarily the shortest ones possible, but are chosen for their clarity and ease of use. Displayed numbers are truncated (not rounded) to two decimal places. If a number is significant, it is shown in the DIS-PLAY column, and its meaning is given in the COMMENT column. Abbreviations are used, and representative cases are shown below.

Abbreviation		*Meaning*
D.d		*Days and decimal part*
	or	*Degrees and decimal part*
.d		*Decimal part of day or degree*
H.h		*Hours and decimal part*
.h		*Decimal part of hour*
M.m		*Minutes and decimal part (angle or time)*
.m		*Decimal part of minute*

Conversion of Time and Angles

When times are given in hours, minutes, and seconds, they must be converted to decimal form for use on the calculator. (An exception is the HP-45, a more expensive machine which can work directly in these units.) The same applies to angles in degrees, minutes, and seconds. The conversion can be done conveniently by storing the conversion constant 60 in the memory, using the STO key to enter it and the RCL key to retrieve it for use. Answers obtained in decimal time or angle must be converted back to familiar form.

Example 24: Convert 7h 31m 08s into decimal form.

MACHINE: *HP35*

KEY	DISPLAY	COMMENT
60 STO		
8		
RCL ÷	*.13*	*.m*
31 +	*31.13*	*M.m*
RCL ÷	*.51*	*.h*
7 +	*7.51*	*H.h*

Ans. 7.51 hours

MACHINE: _SR50_

KEY	DISPLAY	COMMENT
60 STO		
8		
÷ RCL		
+ 31		
=	31.13	M.m
÷ RCL		
+ 7		
=	7.51	H.h

Ans. 7.51h

Example 25: Convert 4.76 hours into hours, minutes, and seconds.

MACHINE: _HP35_

KEY	DISPLAY	COMMENT
60 STO		
4.76 ↑	4.76	H.h, write 4h
4–	.76	.h
RCL x	45.6	M.m, write 45m
45–		
RCL x	36	s, write 36s

Ans. 4h 45m 36s

MACHINE: _SR50_

KEY	DISPLAY	COMMENT
60 STO		
4.76	4.76	H.h, write 4h
–4		
=	.76	.h
x RCL		
=	45.6	M.m, write 45m
–45		
=	.6	.m
x RCL		
=	36	s, write 36s

Ans. 4h 45m 36s

Example 26: Convert 71°32′ into decimal form.

MACHINE: *HP35*

KEY	DISPLAY	COMMENT
		60 still in memory
32		
RCL ÷	*.53*	*.d*
71 +	*71.53*	*D.d*

Ans. 71°.53

MACHINE: *SR50*

KEY	DISPLAY	COMMENT
		60 still in memory
71		
+ 31		
÷ RCL		
=	*71.53*	*D.d*

Ans. 71°.53

Example 27: Convert 38°.515 into degrees, minutes, and tenths. Remember that 60 is still in the memory.

MACHINE: *HP35*

KEY	DISPLAY	COMMENT
38.515 ↑	*38.515*	*D.d, write 38°*
38 −	*.51*	*.d*
RCL x	*30.9*	*M.m, write 30′.9*

Ans. 38°30′.9

MACHINE: *SR50*

KEY	DISPLAY	COMMENT
38.515	*38.515*	*D.d, write 38°*
−38		
=	*.51*	*.d*
x RCL		
=	*30.9*	*M.m, write 30′.9*

Ans. 38°30′.9

Time-Speed-Distance

These problems use the same basic equations given in the previous section: $D = S \times T$ $S = D/T$ $T = D/S$
The solutions are more direct on scientific calculators, especially where time conversions are involved.

Example 28: What distance is covered in 5 hours at 3.3 knots?

	MACHINE: *HP35*			MACHINE: *SR50*	
KEY	**DISPLAY**	**COMMENT**	**KEY**	**DISPLAY**	**COMMENT**
5↑			5		
3.3x	16.5	*Ans. 16.5 n.m.*	x3.3		
			=	16.5	*Ans. 16.5 n.m.*

Example 29: What distance is covered in 3h 28m at a speed of 4.7 knots?

	MACHINE: *HP35*			MACHINE: *SR50*	
KEY	**DISPLAY**	**COMMENT**	**KEY**	**DISPLAY**	**COMMENT**
28↑			3		
60÷	.46	.h	+28		
3+	3.46	H.h	÷RCL		
4.7x	16.29	*Ans. 16.29 n.m.*	=	3.46	H.h
			x4.7		
			=	16.29	*Ans. 16.29 n.m.*

Example 30: What is your speed if you cover 64 miles in 4h 07m?

MACHINE: *HP35*

KEY	DISPLAY	COMMENT
60 STO		
64↑		
7↑	7	M
RCL ÷	.11	.h
4 +	4.11	H.h
÷	15.54	$\dfrac{64}{4.11}$

Ans. 15.54 knots (power boat, obviously!)

MACHINE: *SR50*

KEY	DISPLAY	COMMENT
60 STO		
4		
+ 7		
÷ RCL		
=	4.11	H.h
STO		store time
64		
÷ RCL		
=	15.54	Ans. 15.54 knots

Example 31: How long will it take to travel 210 miles at 6.2 knots?

MACHINE: *HP35*

KEY	DISPLAY	COMMENT
210↑		60 still in STO
6.2÷	33.87	H.h, write 33h
33–	.87	.h
RCL x	52.25	M.m, write 52m

Ans. 33h 52m

MACHINE: *SR50*

KEY	DISPLAY	COMMENT
210		60 still in STO
÷6.2		
=	33.87	H.h, write 33h
–33		
=	.87	.h
x RCL		
=	52.25	M.m, write 52m

Ans. 33h 52m

Example 32: At 11:47 your taffrail log reads 31.8 miles. At 15:21 it reads 46.2 miles. What speed have you been making through the water? The solution here is

$$S = \frac{D_2 - D_1}{T_2 - T_1} = \frac{46.2 - 31.8}{15:21 - 11:47}$$

MACHINE: _HP35_

KEY	DISPLAY	COMMENT
60 STO _ _ _ _		
46.2 ↑		
31.8 —	14.4	$D_2 - D_1$
21		
RCL ÷		
15 +	15.35	T_2 (H.h)
47		
RCL ÷		
11 +	11.78	T_1 (H.h)
—	3.56	$T_2 - T_1$ (H.h)
÷	4.03	Speed=4.03 knots

MACHINE: _SR50_

KEY	DISPLAY	COMMENT
60 STO _ _ _ _		
15		
+ 21		
÷RCL		
−11		
−47		
÷RCL		
=	3.56	$T_2 - T_1$
STO		
46.2		
−31.8		
=	14.4	$D_2 - D_1$
÷RCL		
=	4.03	Ans. 4.03 knots

Time and Angles

Addition and subtraction of time and angles can be done with the same dummy zero method as on four function machines. The work can be done more directly on a scientific calculator by using the memory to store the conversion factor of 60, so that you convert each number to decimal form before adding or subtracting it, and then convert the answer from decimal form back to minutes and seconds.

Example 33: Find the sum of 27m 33s   ①
4m 48s   ②
1m 25s   ③

MACHINE: *HP35*

KEY	DISPLAY	COMMENT
60 STO _ _ _ _		
33 RCL ÷	*.55*	
27 +	*27.55*	① *M.m*
48 RCL ÷	*.8*	
4 +	*4.8*	② *M.m*
+	*32.35*	① + ②
25 RCL ÷	*.41*	
1 +	*1.41*	③ *M.m*
+	*33.76*	*M.m, write 33m*
33–	*.76*	*.m*
RCL x	*46.00*	*.m → s, write 46s*

Ans. 33m 46s

MACHINE: *SR50*

KEY	DISPLAY	COMMENT
60 STO _ _ _		
27		
+ 33 ÷ RCL		
+ 4		
+ 48 ÷ RCL		
+ 1		
+ 25 ÷ RCL		
=	*33.76*	*M.m, write 33m*
–33		
=	*–.76*	*.m*
x RCL		
=	*46.00*	*.m → s, write 46s*

Ans. 33m 46s

Example 34: Find 14m 10s ①
+ 12m 53s ②
— 5m 21s ③

MACHINE: *HP35*

KEY	DISPLAY	COMMENT
60 STO		
10 RCL ÷	*.16*	
14 +	*14.16*	① →*M.m*
53 RCL ÷	*.88*	
12 +	*12.88*	② →*M.m*
+	*27.05*	① + ②
21 RCL ÷	*.35*	
5 +	*5.35*	③ →*M.m*
—	*21.7*	① + ② — ③ *write 21m*
21 —	*.7*	*.m*
RCL x	*42*	*.m →s write 42s*

Ans. 21m 42s

MACHINE: *SR50*

KEY	DISPLAY	COMMENT
60 STO		
14		
+ 10 ÷ RCL		
+ 12		
+ 53 ÷ RCL		
–5		
–21 ÷ RCL		
=	*21.7*	*write 21m*
–21		
=	*.7*	
x RCL		
=	*42*	*write 42s*

Ans. 21m 42s

Taking the average of a number of times or angles is a simple extension of the above method. Find the total of the figures in decimal form. Divide by the number of figures, and then convert back to minutes and seconds, or degrees and minutes.

Example 35: Find the average time for sights taken at 10h 25m 05s ①

10h 25m 42s ②

10h 26m 00s ③

10h 26m 20s ④

Since the hour figure for all the times is 10, we can leave this out of the solution and replace it at the end of the work.

MACHINE: *HP35*

KEY	DISPLAY	COMMENT
5 RCL ÷		
25 +	25.08	① M.m
42 RCL ÷	.7	
25 +	25.7	②
+	50.78	① + ②
26 +	76.78	① + ② + ③
20 RCL ÷	.33	
26 +	26.33	④
+	103.11	① + ② + ③ + ④
4 ÷	25.77	Average in M.m
		write 25m
25–	.77	.m
RCL x	46.75	write 47s

Ans. 10h 25m 47s

MACHINE: *SR50*

KEY	DISPLAY	COMMENT
60 STO		
25		
+ 5 ÷ RCL		
+ 25		
+ 42 ÷ RCL		
+ 26		
+ 26		
+ 20 ÷ RCL		
=	*103.11*	*total time M.m*
÷ 4		
=	*25.77*	*average time M.m*
		write 25m
−25		
=	*.77*	
x RCL		
=	*46.75*	*write 47s*

Ans. 25m 47s

Solution of the Navigational Triangle

Earlier in the book, sight reduction tables were used to determine the sun's altitude (Hc) and azimuth angle (Z) as would be seen at an assumed position (AP). Let's review the process briefly. The sun's GP is known, and we choose an AP. With the latitude of the GP (Dec), the latitude of the AP (aL), and the difference of the two longitudes (MA), we enter the tables to find the values of Hc and Z. Now, it shouldn't surprise anybody to realize that we can also work out these values on a calculator, and so we have an alternative to tables.

I'm as lazy as the next guy, and maybe lazier than his brother, but I haven't traded in my tables on a calculator yet. And I'm not about to. For one thing, I *like* using tables. It's a simple, comfortable routine requiring no thought on a cold wet night. For another, salt water is notably hostile to delicate mechanisms, and I think a sealed plastic bag would be the only safe place for a calculator at sea. For another, a few dollars for a sight reduction table sure beats a couple of hundred for a scientific calculator. Finally, and this will be a hard blow to calculator fans, the tables are faster. Sitting in a warm dry study, I find that solving a typical problem with the tables takes 50 seconds; the same problem on a calculator takes 1 minute 35 seconds. On board a lively boat, with cold hands, the difference would be much more, especially if I had to stop to look up the equations. Which I would. For average work, then, tables are still the answer. I'm giving the calculator solutions here because they're interesting examples of the power and flexibility of a scientific calculator, and because they have applications in special situations. A few of these are:

1. Cases where the Declination is outside the range of HO249 tables.

2. Cases where extreme accuracy is required.

3. Situations where the value of Hc is less than $+5°$, when the solution is not found in HO214, or less than $-5°$, when HO249 also fails. These situations can occur in great circle calculations and lunar distance sights for determining the time. HO229 can be used, but it may not be available, and in any case is not very convenient if the entering values are not whole degrees.

Refer to Figure 12-1. The latitude of the AP is L (shortened from aL for simplicity in the equations). Likewise, the Declination of the GP is D, and the meridian angle is M. The calculated azimuth angle is Z. The calculated length (in degrees) of side c, subtracted from $90°$, gives Hc.

The equations are: $Hc = sin^{-1} (sin\ L \cdot sin\ D + cos\ L \cdot cos\ D \cdot cos\ M)$

$$Z = tan^{-1} (\frac{sin\ M}{cos\ L \cdot tan\ D - sin\ L \cdot cos\ M})$$

It's interesting to note that in the days before sight reduction tables, similar equations in logarithmic form were solved longhand.

The equation for Hc is pretty well standard, and was used for calculating most of the HO229 tables. The equation for Z is one of several

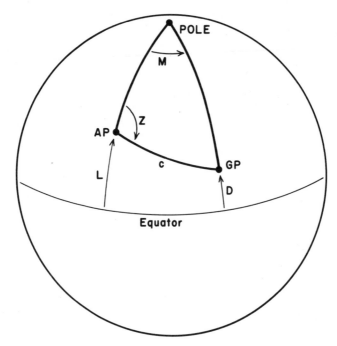

Figure 12-1.

which can be used. It is longer than some, but has the great advantage of eliminating any uncertainty regarding the value of Z. With the other equations, the number obtained is always positive, but it may or may not have to be subtracted from $180°$, according to a cute little set of rules which are next to impossible to remember. With this equation, if the number obtained is positive, it is the value of Z. If it is negative, add $180°$ to obtain Z.

If you choose the AP in the usual way, L and M will be whole degrees, and can be entered in the calculator without any fuss. D, however, will generally not be a whole degree, and must be converted from degrees and minutes into decimal degrees. To avoid doing this more than once, we will do it first and store the decimal value in memory.

Also note that when solving for Z, we will begin with the denominator. In theory, the general method of using scientific calculators would let us begin with the numerator, but in fact there isn't quite enough register capacity.

Example 36: For the sun sight at the front of the book, L = 42°N, D = 16°05′ Same Name, and M = 23°E. Find Hc and Z.

MACHINE: *HP35*

KEY	DISPLAY	COMMENT
5 ↑ 60 ÷ 16 +	16.08	*Dec in D.d*
STO		*save for re-use*
42 sin		
RCL sin		
x	.18	*1st term*
42 cos		
RCL cos		
x		
23 cos		
x	.65	*2nd term*
+	.84	*1st + 2nd terms*
Arc sin	57.42	*Hc in D.d, write 57°*
57−	.42	*.d*
60x	25.36	*Round off to 25′*
		Hc = 57°25′
42 cos		*For Z, start with denom.*
RCL tan		
x	.21	*1st term*
42 sin		
23 cos		
x	.61	*2nd term*
−	−.40	*denominator (d)*
1/x	−2.48	$\dfrac{1}{d}$
23 sin	.39	*numerator (n)*
x	−.97	$n \times \dfrac{1}{d} \;=\; \dfrac{n}{d}$
Arc tan	−44.20	
180 +	135.79	*round off to 136°*

Ans. Hc = 57°25′

Z = N136°E

Example 36:

MACHINE: <u>SR50</u>

KEY	DISPLAY	COMMENT
16		
+ 5 ÷ 60		
=	16.08	*Dec in D.d*
STO		*Save for re-use*
42 sin		
x		
RCL sin		
+	.18	*1st term*
42 cos		
x		
RCL cos		
x		
23 cos		
=	.84	*1st + 2nd term*
Arc sin	57.42	*Hc in D.d; write 57°*
−57		
=	.42	
x 60		
=	25.36	*write 25'*
42 cos		
x		
RCL tan		
−	.21	*1st term of denominator*
42 sin		
x		
23 cos		
=	−.40	*denominator*
1/x		
x		
23 sin		
=	−.97	
Arc tan	−44.2	
+ 180		
=	135.79	*round off to 136*

Ans. Hc = 57°25'

Z = N136°E

In the previous example, the Declination was the same name as latitude. When the Declination is contrary name, it must be entered in memory as a negative number. This is done with the CH S key or the +/− key, whichever your machine has.

Example 37:   In the sight on page 56, L = 29°S, D = 19°23′ Contrary Name, and M = 66°W. Find Hc and Z.

Example 37:

MACHINE: *HP35*

KEY	DISPLAY	COMMENT
23 ↑ 60 ÷ 19 +		
CH S STO	*−19.38*	*Dec in D.d*
29 sin		
RCL sin		
x	*−.16*	*1st term*
29 cos		
RCL cos		
x		
66 cos		
x	*.33*	*2nd term*
+	*.17*	*1st + 2nd terms*
Arc sin	*10.05*	*Hc in D.d; write 10°*
10−	*.05*	
60 x	*3.58*	*round off, write 04′*
29 cos		*start with denominator*
RCL tan		
x	*−.30*	*1st term*
29 sin		
66 cos		
x	*.19*	*2nd term*
−	*−.50*	*denom.*
1/x	*−1.98*	
66 sin	*.91*	*numerator*
x	*1.80*	*Num. ÷ Denom.*
Arc tan	*−61.071*	
180 +	*118.92*	*round off to 119°*

Ans. Hc = 10°04′
Z = S119°W

Occasionally you will need to calculate Hc and Z for a situation where none of the entering values are whole degrees. This can occur when you want Hc for a DR position, rather than an assumed position. It is also common in great circle work. HO249 tables do not provide the solution for these cases. HO214 and HO229 do allow for interpolation by means of auxiliary tables and graphs, respectively. They aren't the most convenient things to use, though, especially the latter. The solution can be found directly on the calculator, by storing the conversion constant 60, and converting each angle to decimal form as you use it. This sounds complicated, and the sequences below look long, but actually they fall into a routine and are almost as fast as solutions for whole degree cases.

Example 38: In solving a star sight from a DR position, you have L = $45°12'$N, D = $21°52'$ Same Name, and M = $85°34'$W. Find Hc and Z.

MACHINE: *HP35*

KEY	DISPLAY	COMMENT
60 STO		
12 RCL ÷ 45 +	45.2	
sin	.70	
52 RCL ÷ 21 +	21.86	
sin	.37	
x	.26	1st term
12 RCL ÷ 45 +	45.2	
cos	.70	
52 RCL ÷ 21 +	21.86	
cos	.92	
x	.65	
34 RCL ÷ 85 +	85.56	
cos	.07	
x	.05	2nd term
+	.31	1st + 2nd terms
Arc sin	18.35	Hc in D.d, write 18°
18 – 60 x	21.02	write 21'
12 RCL ÷ 45 +	45.2	
cos	.70	
52 RCL ÷ 21 +	21.86	
tan	.40	
x	.28	1st term denom.
12 RCL ÷ 45 +	45.2	
sin	.70	
34 RCL ÷ 85 +	85.56	
cos	.07	
x	.05	2nd term denom.
–	.22	denom.
1/x	4.38	
34 RCL ÷ 85 +	85.56	
sin	.99	numerator
x	4.37	num. ÷ denom.
arc tan	77.12	round to 77°

Ans. Hc = $18°21'$ Z = N$77°$W

PRACTICE PROBLEMS

1. 10h 43m 38s
 + 2h 28m 51s

2. 157°43′.3
 − 2°17′.8

3. 12h 46m 38s
 − 11m 42s

4. 126°42′
 + 8°39′
 + 14′

5. Average 49m 45s
 50m 20s
 50m 40s
 51m 00s

6. Average 31°07′
 31°03′
 30°59′
 30°55′

7. Convert 12.34 hours into hours, minutes, and seconds.

8. If you travel 135 miles in 20h 36m, what is your speed?

9. In reducing a sun sight, you have L = 45°N
 D = 17°23′ Same Name
 M = 31°E
Find Hc and Z.

10. For a star sight, you have L = 37°10′S
 D = 5°21′, Contrary Name
 M = 45°50′W
Find Hc and Z.

Answers to these problems are in the Appendix.

Appendix

ANSWERS TO PRACTICE PROBLEMS

CHAPTER 3. THE SEXTANT

1. hs $52°17'$
    IC $-05'$
    Dip $-03'$
    App. Alt. $52°09'$
    Ref-SD $+15'$
    Ho $52°24'$

2. hs $22°57'$
    IC $+02'$
    Dip $-03'$
    App. Alt. $22°56'$
    Ref-SD $+14'$
    Ho $23°10'$

3. hs $72°35'$
    IC $-04'$
    Dip $-03'$
    App. Alt. $72°28'$
    Ref-SD $-16'$
    Ho $72°12'$

4. hs $08°27'$
    IC $+11'$
    Dip $-02'$
    App. Alt. $08°36'$
    Ref-SD $+10'$
    Ho $08°46'$

CHAPTER 6. THE NAUTICAL ALMANAC

1.

	GHA	Dec
18d 03h	225°55′	19°30′N
32m 05s	8°01′	+0′
	233°56′	19°30′N

2.

	GHA	Dec
16d 19h	105°55′	19°12′N
33m 40s	8°25′	+0′
	114°20′	19°12′N

3.

	GHA	Dec
17d 12h	0°55′	19°22′N
33m 27s	8°22′	+0′
	9°17′	19°22′N

4.

	GHA	Dec
16d 05h	255°56′	19°04′N
32m 16s	8°04′	+0′
	264°00′	19°04′N

CHAPTER 7. SIGHT REDUCTION TABLES

1. aL   45°N
   aλ   53°23′W
   MA   84°W

2. aL   27°N
   aλ   130°19′E
   MA   81°W

3. aL   65°S
   aλ   160°35′W
   MA   40°E

4. aL   33°N
   aλ   140°22′E
   MA   77°E

5. Tab Hc   73°47′   d+38′   Z S125E
          +11′
      Hc   73°58′

6. Tab Hc   22°31′   d-39′   Z N123W
          -05′
      Hc   22°26′

7. Tab Hc   60°53′   d+22′   Z N99W
          +18′
      Hc   61°11′

8. Tab Hc   24°00′   d-42′   Z S129E
          -26′
      Hc   23°34′

CHAPTER 9. LINES OF POSITION AT SEA

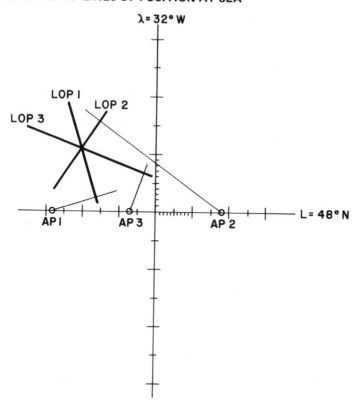

CHAPTER 10. MOON, PLANET, AND STAR SIGHTS

1.

	GHA	v	Dec	d
16d 14h	219°06′	+12.0	21°09′S	+6.7
56m 13s	13°25′			
	+11′		+06′	
	232°42′		21°15′S	

2. hs   20°43′   H.P. 54.4
       IC   −03′
       Dip   −03′
   App Alt 20°37′
             +62′
             +01′
             −30′ (UL)
    Ho   21°10′

3.

	GHA	v	Dec	d
20d 18h 33m 02s	224°43'	+2.6	17°57'S	+.1
	8°16'			
	+02'		+0'	
	233°01'		17°57'S	

4. 19d 01h   282°07'
       57m 04s   14°18'
              146°23'   19°19'N Dec
              442°48'
         - 360°00'
            82°48' GHA

CHAPTER 11. OTHER SIGHT REDUCTION TABLES

1. Alt   64°26' Δd +.92 Az N150E
           +11'
   Hc   64°37'

CHAPTER 12. PORTABLE CALCULATORS

1. 13h 12m 29s
2. 155°25'.5
3. 12h 34m 56s
4. 135°35'
5. 50m 26s
6. 31°01'
7. 12h 20m 24s
8. 6.55 knots
9. Hc = 52°09'   Z = N127°E
10. Hc = 29°46'   Z = S125°W

STAR CHARTS

NORTHERN STARS

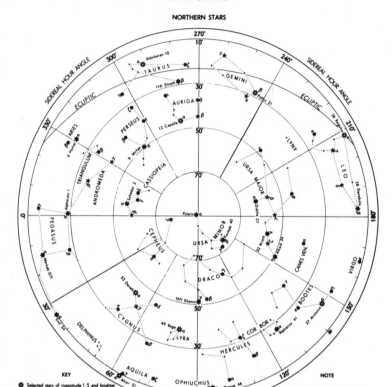

KEY

✵ Selected stars of magnitude 1·5 and brighter
✸ Selected stars of magnitude 1·6 and fainter
★ Other tabulated stars of magnitude 2·5 and brighter
● Other tabulated stars of magnitude 2·6 and fainter
· Untabulated stars

NOTE

The numbers enclosed in brackets refer to those stars of the selected list which are not used in H.O. 249 (A.P. 3270).

EQUATORIAL STARS (S.H.A. 0° to 180°)

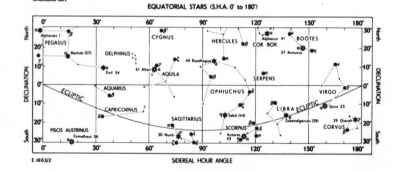

E.1663/2   SIDEREAL HOUR ANGLE

STAR CHARTS

SOUTHERN STARS

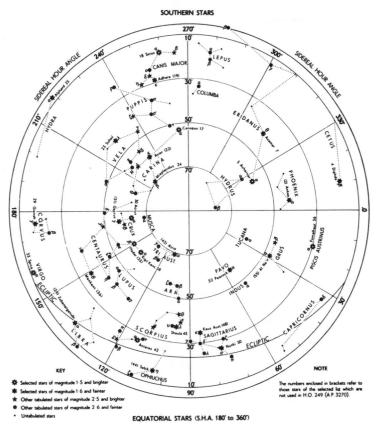

KEY

✿ Selected stars of magnitude 1·5 and brighter
✪ Selected stars of magnitude 1·6 and fainter
★ Other tabulated stars of magnitude 2·5 and brighter
● Other tabulated stars of magnitude 2·6 and fainter
· Untabulated stars

NOTE

The numbers enclosed in brackets refer to those stars of the selected list which are not used in H.O. 249 (A.P. 3270).

EQUATORIAL STARS (S.H.A. 180° to 360°)

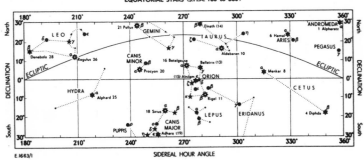

E.1663/1   SIDEREAL HOUR ANGLE

141

Glossary

Altitude (Alt.):   The angle from the horizon to the body observed.

Apparent Altitude (App. Alt.):   The measured altitude after applying corrections for index error and dip.

Assumed Latitude (aL):   The latitude of the assumed position, chosen for convenience in using sight reduction tables.

Assumed Longitude (aλ):   The longitude of the assumed position.

Assumed Position (AP):   A position close to the actual or dead reckoning position, arbitrarily chosen for convenience in using sight reduction tables.

Azimuth (Zn):   The true bearing of the body observed, measured from north clockwise through $360°$, in the fashion of a compass rose.

Azimuth Angle (Z or Az):   The true bearing of the body observed, measured from either north or south, toward either east or west, through $180°$. This is one of the figures obtained from sight reduction tables.

Course Made Good (CMG):   The course, or bearing, from an initial point to a final point, without regard to the intervening travel.

Dead Reckoning (DR):   Originally called *deduced reckoning,* for the method of deducing progress from known courses and speeds.

Declination (Dec):   The angle measured from the equator, north or south to the geographic position of the body observed.

Distance Made Good (DMG): The distance between an initial point and a final point, without regard to the intervening travel.

Dip (D): Depression of the apparent horizon below a truly horizontal plane. The term is usually applied to the negative correction rather than the error itself.

Estimated Position (EP): A position obtained basically by dead reckoning, but probably containing errors from imperfectly known factors such as currents.

Geographic Position (GP): The point on the earth's surface where the observed body is directly overhead, i.e. has an altitude of $90°$ and casts no shadow. The coordinates of the point, GHA and Declination, are listed in the Nautical Almanac for any given instant of time. Sometimes called the ground position or ground point.

Greenwich Hour Angle (GHA): The angle measured from the longitude of Greenwich ($0°$ longitude, or the prime meridian) <u>west</u> to the longitude of the geographic position of the body observed.

Greenwich Mean Time (GMT): A uniform time system without time zones, generally used for celestial navigation.

Height-calculated (Hc): The angle above the horizon, or altitude, of a body, calculated from its geographic position and the observers assumed position. This is one of the figures obtained from sight reduction tables.

Height-observed (Ho): The angle, or altitude, at which the body is actually seen. Ho is obtained from the sextant reading after applying corrections for various errors.

Height-sextant (hs): The reading of the sextant, before applying any corrections.

Horizontal Parallax (HP): A reduction in observed altitude of the surface of the earth, caused by the proximity of the body observed. It is greatest when the body is on the horizon. HP for the moon is large and requires correction. HP for the sun and planets is small and usually neglected. The stars have no measurable HP.

Hour Angle (HA): The angle measured from the longitude of the observer (or the assumed position) <u>east or west</u> through $180°$ to the longitude of the geographic position of the body. Also known as meridian angle. Variously abbreviated as HA or t, and in this book as MA. Older works sometimes called this angle *Local Hour Angle (LHA);* this term now has a different meaning, but is sometimes seen used incorrectly.

Index Correction (IC): The correction applied to the reading of a sextant to allow for its index error.

Index Error: A sextant reading other than zero when a zero angle is observed. This is usually checked with the horizon or a star.

Line of Position (LOP): A line on which the observer is located. In celestial navigation, lines of position are obtained by sextant observation and calculation.

Local Hour Angle (LHA): The angle measured from the longitude of the observer (or the assumed position) <u>westward</u> through 360° to the longitude of the body.

Local Hour Angle of Aries (LHA ♈): Same as above, but measured to the longitude of a point (not a star) known as the Frist Point of Aries.

Lower Limb (LL): The lower edge of the sun or moon. For sun observations, the lower limb is generally used.

Meridian Angle (MA): See Hour Angle.

Refraction: Bending toward the earth of the light rays from a celestial object as they enter the atmosphere.

Refraction Correction (R): A negative correction applied to the apparent altitude.

Refraction-Semidiameter Correction (R-SD): A correction applied to the apparent altitude of the sun's limb. It may be positive or negative, depending on which limb was observed.

Right Ascension (RA): A measurement used in astronomy, and in Nautical Almanacs prior to 1952. It is the angle (expressed in hours of 15°) from the First Point of Aries <u>eastward</u> to the body.

Semidiameter (SD): Half of the angular diameter of the sun or moon, amounting to about 16′ for either. A correction for the semidiameter of the sun or moon is applied to sextant readings. The semidiameter of the planets is neglected. Stars have no measurable semidiameter.

Sidereal Hour Angle (SHA): The angle from the longitude of the First Point of Aries, measured <u>westward</u> through 360° to the body, usually a star. The GHA of a star is found by adding its SHA to the GHA of the First Point of Aries.

Upper Limb (UL): The upper edge of the sun or moon. Its main use is with moon observations.

Index

The navigator of a vessel at Dead Reckoning position 41°57′S, 121°35′E takes a sight of the star Altair. The time of the sight is May 1973, 19d 22h 18m 56s GMT. The measured altitude is 29°28′. The index error is 02′ on the arc, and the height of eye is 15 feet.

1973 May 19d 22h 18m 56s

1973 May	GHA	Dec
19d 22h	207°26′	
18m 56s	4°45′	
Altair	62°37′	8°48′N
	274°48′	8°48′N

Altair hs   29°28′
        IC   -02′
        Dip   -04′
        App. Alt. 29°22′
        R   -02′
        Ho   29°20′

aλ   121°12′E   Tab Dec   8° Contrary
MA   36°W   Tab Hc   30°09′   d – 52′   Z S138°W
aL   42°S   cor   -42′
                 Hc   29°27′   a = 7A

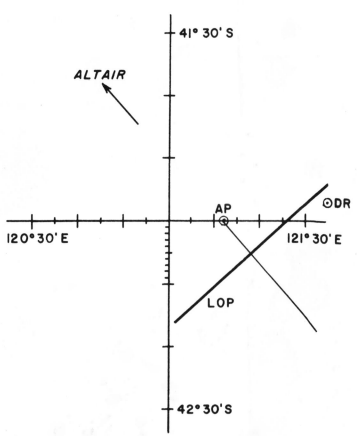